PRINCETON THEOLOGICAL MONOGRAPH SERIES

Dikran Y. Hadidian

General Editor

11

FREEDOM AND CIVILIZATION AMONG THE GREEKS

2217   2-5-92

FREEDOM
AND
CIVILIZATION
AMONG THE
GREEKS

By

A.-J Festugière, O.P.

Translated by

P. T. Brannan, S.J.

PICKWICK PUBLICATIONS
Allison Park, Pennsylvania

Originally published as
Liberté et civilisation chez les Grecs.
© 1947 by Editions de la Revue des Jeunes

Copyright © 1987 by Pickwick Publications
4137 Timberlane Drive, Allison Park, PA 15101

Library of Congress Cataloging-in-Publication Data

Festugière, A.-J. (André Jean), 1898-1982
    Freedom and civilization among the Greeks.

    (Princeton theological monograph series ; 11)
    Translation of: Liberté et civilisation chez les Grecs
    1. Greece--Politics and government. 2. Civilization,
Greek. 3. Liberty. I. Title. II. Series.
JC73. F4313 1987   323.44' 0937   87-7809
ISBN 0-915138-98-0

CONTENTS

INTRODUCTION

Freedom is more than a word, more than the base coinage
Of statesmen, the tyrant's dishonoured cheque, or the dreamer's mad
Inflated currency. She is mortal, we know, and made
In the image of simple men who have no taste for carnage
But sooner kill and are killed than see that image betrayed.
Mortal she is, yet risint always refreshed from her ashes:
She is bound to earth, yet she flies as high as a passage bird
To home wherever man's heart with season warmth is stirred:
Innocent in her touch as the dawn's, but still it unleashes
The ravisher shades of envy. Freedom is more than a word.

C. Day-Lewis, *The Nabara*, 1-10

The year 1987, the bicentennial year of the Constitution of the United States of America, is certainly a fitting time to give some consideration to the history of freedom as a philosophical concept and a human and political reality. We claim we owe this precious inheritance to the ancients. What better way to understand it than to see its development in Greece and Rome? In these civilizations freedom is more than a word. It is a hard-won and deeply cherished possession. In Christianity through the Word, Christ, it assumes a more elevated meaning. This brief work traces this evolution.

Words, words, words! We are exposed to so many of them that we frequently forget what they mean. Yet, John Cardinal Newman can remind us that "A word has power to convey a world of information to the imagination, and to act as a spell upon the feelings; there is no need of sustained fiction -- often no room for it." ("Poetry with Reference to Aristotle's *Poetics*," section 3.) We know this, but often either from use or abuse a word can become meaningless or an end in itself. We can find ourselves mesmerized by our own rhetoric, by mere cant. Words which once aroused passionate responses become banal, bathetic; others can become vital and significant, not necessarily in themselves, but because of our own emotional reactions to them. Some which denote most precious realities become stereotypic jargon; others carry value because of connotations and associations. We should not be surprised, then, that in an age as politicized as our own we should have to be reminded of certain values. Words as important as **liberty** and **freedom** can be stripped of meaning or become mere jargon. It is good that poets such as C. Day-Lewis remind us that "Freedom is more than a word," and that scholars such as the Reverend A.-J. Festugière, the French Dominican, explore for us some of the essential characteristics of freedom.

The Context of Festugière's Concern

The history of the composition and publication of the original French studies makes this book particularly interesting: they are dated from 1942 to 1945 and may be readily viewed in the light of the Second World War and the occupation of France when National Socialism and Fascism were proclaiming "liberty," or the freedom and autonomy of the Superman, and Super Race, the freedom of the ruling party. It was in this context that Anouilh presented his adaptation of Sophocles *Antigone*. The French were forced to answer the questions: at what price freedom? Rather than limit or date them, the circumstances give these works immediacy. For the subject under consideration is not any political system, but man himself: basic humanity, fundamental human freedom, the political animal in his natural milieu, civilization. The clear perception is that the city does not give rise to the citizen; the citizens create the city. Man, the social animal, does not exist for the sake of society; society comes to be from, and exists for the sake of man. Society and civilization ultimately derive from, and must ever rest on human nature. All freedom, all rights, all obligations must be seen in the light of this same nature. Such considerations make for a complex picture, but we ignore these complexities at our peril.

This translation represents a collection of some of Father Festugière's observations which were published as a book in 1947 under the title: *Liberté et civilisation chez les Grecs.* It presents a well-rounded understanding of the Classical and Christian foundations of this priceless possession of freedom. Using the sciences of history, philology, philosophy, and theology, Festugiére develops a brief history of the ideal of freedom as it was born, nurtured, and transformed in the West.

Freedom: The Individual and Society

As he started his search for the moral virtue of Justice in the *Republic,* Plato makes Socrates opt for an investigation into the ideal state, since there he would find "writ large" the same virtues found in the individual. Plato thus clearly indicated his own conviction that the individual and society were closely linked: one was a microcosm of the other. One of the great contributions of Ancient Greece to civilization was this gradually developing realization that freedom is a possession of the individual human soul, and that it belongs to it by nature. Freedom is not conferred by a particular state, or city, or class. True, external freedom might be curtailed, but the freedom of the individual is a given. Recognition of this fact has been a hard-won victory for human nature. It developed slowly but cogently: Plato and Aristotle laid the ground-work, the Stoics and Epicureans gave it very practical application; it was transplanted to Rome where, under the nurturing of the Neoplatonists and Christianity, it grew into the Christian concept of human dignity.

Man who found his perfection in society was, the Greek noted, to an extent limited by the same society. His freedom had to be exercised within a framework; he had to be civilized. But beyond this relationship to his fellowmen, Christians emphasized man's relationship with God. Freedom or liberty was seen as a relational word on several levels. Man is free **from** something and **for** something. Society liberates him from certain cares to be free for other pursuits and for other people. Christianity introduced a new level: liberation from sin and death to be free to live for God, as St. Paul expresses it. St. Augustine of Hippo with characteristic rhetorical flair summed up this new freedom in a few pithy and memorable expressions: 1) before the redemption wrought by Christ man was fundamentally in the position where *non possum non peccare* (I cannot not sin); 2) by the grace of Christ he is freed from this servitude to the freedom where *possum non peccare* (I can not sin) and, therefore, *possum peccare* (I can sin); 3) by proper use

ix

of this freedom from sin man is lead to the ultimate freedom where *non possum peccare* (I cannot sin) because man has entered into the eternal beatitude of the blessed where he is perfectly united with the will of God. Hence St. Augustine's famous definition of freedom: being in the state where we can do what we ought to do. The ultimate freedom or liberty of the sons and daughters of God can only be obtained hereafter. Meanwhile, we still have the power, through the grace of Christ, to do what we should do. Again we have a complex picture and complex relationships.

The ideal of freedom, then is found to consist in man's ability to function as he should. The free man is one who can satisfy the demands of human nature. This is a sublime ideal, but we are only too aware of the enormous questions it poses. (For example, what is human nature?) In the tradition we follow here, it is clear that freedom cannot be absolute. Absolute freedom, as proclaimed by many moderns, is the figment of incurably romantic minds, of existential dreamers. Freedom, of its very nature, involves relationships and is exercised in society. It further involves politics, laws, rights, duties, and many other personal elements. It ultimately involves values and, therefore, morality. The complexity only increases.

Anarchy and Anomie

At the beginning of recorded political thought in the West one thing is clear: absolute freedom or liberty really implied *anarchia* (anarchy, literally a state of no government or control) a chaotic state in which there is no real freedom. If everyone is his own law, there is no law *(anomia)*. If there is no law, there is not order. If there is not order, there is no peace. Order facilitates man's exercise of freedom. Regulations are needed here and now that man may live civilly. Perhaps in another world man might be able to live differently. In heaven, for example, the blessed live without external law, for the will of God is their only delight and goal. In this world man needs law and order to preserve his freedom.

We however, live at a time when the concept of freedom or liberty has become quite confused. We fail to distinguish between civil liberty and natural liberty. We think that because we are constitutionally, that is, legally free to do something, we are also morally free to do it. Modern man often gives the impression that freedom means the ability and right to be or to do whatever he wants, whenever he wants. Such an approach is ultimately frustrating, because it is both unrealistic and unnatural. The twentieth century is itself a limitation. We are not free to live with Plato, Christ, Michelangelo. Our lives are conditioned to an extent by origin, race, nation. All these determinations are limitations, but not necessarily drawbacks or evils. Because I am a human being, I do not have the natural ability to fly as a bird. Were I to claim that this lack deprives me of a basic freedom -- I cannot soar like an eagle -- I would be fatuous. Similarly, I am male. Therefore, I cannot naturally be a mother. All protests against this reality are both futile and stupid. I cannot reasonably or honestly decry my inability to conceive as an act of injustice or a limitation of my rights. Males are not made that way. Perhaps I would rather have it otherwise, but such wishful thinking, has nothing to do with reality. All my protestations -- and even machinations -- will not change the basic reality and nature of mankind.

All decision or choice involves further limitation. When a man chooses to marry, he assumes certain rights which he cannot justly be denied, but he also undertakes certain obligations which restrict his freedom. It is unreal and unreasonable for a married man to live, think, and act as if he were a bachelor. I am not saying that men cannot live this way because *de facto* they are doing so, and *contra factum non valet illatio*. The point is: at what expense are they living this way? What harvest is society reaping from this approach to so-called freedom and personal rights? What are the repercussions on the "liberated" as they experience tensions, frustrations, and alienations? We have to learn to accept the nature of things: we are inherently limited, and our choices involve further limitations. Since our choices are exercises of freedom, our limitations should be seen as freely chosen.

False Liberalism

There are limits to our freedom, limits which derive from various sources, including our basic nature as well as our own choices. Some, however, might concede this point and still maintain that freedom of thought is an absolute. It is true that one cannot keep another from thinking what he will, but my freedom to think what ever I want to think does not mean that I thereby change reality. Rational thought too, is limited by the real and the possible. A madman is free to think that he is Napoleon, but his thought does not transform him into Napoleon. We thank God for our leaps of fancy, for our works of fantasy and imagination, but we still rejoice to keep the real distinct from the whimsical. Even freedom of thought has limits -- if it is to remain reasonable.

John Henry Cardinal Newman addressed this issue in "Note A" of his *Apologia Pro Vita Sua*. Because of the ambiguity of the term, he wishes to establish what he means by "liberalism." Two men, whom he respects, Count Montalembert and Father Lacordaire, are both called liberals, and he notes:

> I do not believe that it is possible for me to differ in any important matter from two men whom I so highly admire. In their general line of thought and conduct I enthusiastically concur, and consider them to be before their age. . . . If I hesitate to adopt their language about Liberalism, I impute the necessity of such to some differences between us in the use of words or in the circumstances of country; and thus I reconcile myself to remaining faithful to my own conception of it, though I cannot have their voices to give force to mine.

The liberalism that concerns Newman is what he found at work at Oxford during the University reforms of the early nineteenth century. It manifested itself in men who would be considered "as being an honour indeed to Oxford, but withal exposed to the temptation of ambitious views, and to the spiritual evils signified in what is called the 'pride of reason.' " The reform movement involved what Newman called "the normal malady incident to such a pursuit." He adds: "In this select circle or class of men, in various Colleges, the direct instruments and the choice fruit of real University Reform, we see the rudiments of the liberal party."

Newman explains his position:

> Whenever men are able to act at all, there is the chance of extreme and intemperate action, and therefore, when there is exercise of mind, there is the chance of wayward or mistaken exercise. Liberty of thought is in itself a good; but it gives an opening to false liberty. Now by Liberalism

I mean false liberty of thought or the exercise of thought upon matter, in which, from the constitution of the human mind, thought cannot be brought to any successful issue, and therefore is out of place. Among such matters are first principles of whatever kind; and of these the most sacred and momentous are especially to be reckoned the truths of Revelation. Liberalism then is the mistake of subjecting to human judgment those revealed doctrines which are in their nature beyond and independent of it, amd of claiming to determine on intrinsic grounds the truth and value of propositions which rest for their reception simply on the external authority of the Divine Word.

Newman was, of course, concerned with liberalism as it manifested itself in the academic and religious world of his day. His point, however, is clear and is applicable to any discussion of freedom of thought. All thought must be reasonable. Thought cannot be successfully exercised on "first principles of whatever kind." St. Thomas Aquinas mentions that there are such things as silly or stupid questions. For example, why is man a rational animal? The only intelligent answer is because that is what a man is and that is how God made him. Were a man not to be a rational animal, he would not be a man. All this may sound like double-talk, but the fact of the matter is that we must start somewhere. We may intelligently ask: What is this thing? How does it work? What should it do? where does it come from? Where is it going? But to ask "Why is a rational animal a man?" or "Why isn't this rational animal a tree?" is to play games with reason and reality. We have data which we must accept. We may, indeed, question whether a being is a human being, but once we have established that it is such, we know that it is a rational animal. (A case in point: if scientists can prove that baboons are rational animals, we have another great field for evangelization.) Many may not accept this approach to reality, but it is reasonable and affords a foundation for rational discourse.

Ultimately the insistence on freedom from all limitations characterizes the thorough-going liberal. Such a mentality is coincident with nihilism, because it demands the denial of, and even the destruction of all data. Bazarov, Turgenev's nihilist in *Fathers and Sons,* comes to mind:

> "We believe in whatever we consider useful," Bazarov said. "These days negation is more useful than anything else -- so

we negate."

"Everything?"

"Yes, everything."

"What? Not only art, poetry, but even. . .itis too shocking to utter. . . . "

Pavel Petrovich stared at him. He had not expected this. Arkady, on the other hand, flushed with pleasure.

"But, look here," Nikolai Petrovich broke in. "You negate everything, or, to be more exact, you destroy everything. But who is going to do the building?"

"That's not our affair. The ground has to be cleared first."

This mentality characterized much of the nineteenth-century liberalism that fully exercised the mind of Cardinal Newman. It is the mentality apotheosized by Friedrich Nietzsche and popularized by many twentieth-century existentialists. It is not just the vigorous rejection of all external values to stress the individual and the will to power as proclaimed by Nietzsche. It is also the attitude preached and insinuated by Sartre and others: that beings and values owe their authentic existence to individual acceptance alone. They are, if you will, our own creations. These same principles are found in the Marxism of a Herbert Marcuse and were incarnated in the radicalism of his student Angela Davis in the late sixties and early seventies. They are seen more subtly, and certainly more insidiously in the heroes of Rand. It is a pervasive attitude, common to all these authors, to deny all values except their own convictions as long as they remain convictions. There is a fundamental denial of reality in itself and the passionate affirmation of individual freedom to negate or create at will. The nineteenth-century liberal, who has become the twentieth-century "Superman" or secular humanist, delights in sweeping away thousands of years of civilization. Like Bazarov, he is frequently unconcerned about what to put in its place. When he has a substitute, it is all too frequently either rank personalism or impersonal community. But, man by his nature demands a combination of both, and ultimately such is true civilization.

Normally, however, even the "liberal" must recognize the

need for some limits as he asserts **his own rights** -- whatever their source may be -- to be free from all law and to ride roughshod over **the rights of others,** which he maintains are non-existent. This stance is, of course, inherently contradictory, but the tradition of reason and reality makes no sense to the anarchist or nihilist. No person has value in himself. Nothing has value in itself. They are all means to an arbitrary end. Even society and civilization are meaningless in themselves since they exist only to be manipulated towards the achievement of a personally conceived and individually satisfying goal or good. The authentic anarchist must view even himself as a mere means to his ideal in the pursuit of which all things, even himself, may be legitimately sacrificed. There is a fanatical consistency in this approach, but it can hardly be called reasonable and just. It is difficult to equate such thought with any intelligent understanding of freedom or liberty.

The fundamental point in this entire discussion is simple enough: if an individual asserts his own freedom and its concomitant rights, he must be prepared to grant the same freedom and rights to other human beings. Every right begets duty. What I claim for myself as a human being, I must be prepared to grant to others. Conflicts will arise. They will have to be settled justly as we attempt to preserve as much liberty as kpossible for all. In keeping with right reason, we know that we cannot realistically be free to do the impossible on any level of merely human existence. We know that we can pervert the right order of things, but there is hope as long as we recognize the perversion. If, however, the Superman with all of his Nietzschean attributes is substituted for the real order, then all talk of rights and freedom is illusory. Here, I submit, is where the questions lay when Festugiére engaged in these studies. Here also some forty years later in a different world the questions lies now. It is the ever-old and ever-new question, the question Socrates, Plato, and Aristotle faced in the fifth and fourth centuries before Christ, and answered on a basically human level. Their answer, founded on the brotherhood of man, gave life and spirit to the civilizations of Greece and rome which then permeated the Western world. With Christ, this brotherhood received a transcendental foundation in the Fatherhood of God. The foundation of our liberty as the followers of Christ, as Christians, is not just our humanity, but the fact that we share the same Spirit, can call God "Our Father," and are Sons and Daughters of God, and Brothers and Sisters of Jesus Christ. We live in a new order, simultaneously built upon but transcending the marvellous insights and truths of the Ancients. In this instance it is quite clear why the study and understanding of the Classics are of such importance: they are truly the *Praeparatio Evangelica* (The Preparation for the Good News). In Christ we do not sweep away the past, but build upon it and bring it to perfection.

Finally , a word of gratitude to two people. Miss Rosemary Hudecheck was an energetic and peerless typist who worked wonders from a difficult manuscript and offered much needed advice in matters musical; Father F. F. Burch, S.J., has accompanied this book on every step of its production. I honestly and humbly acknowledge him as a true collaborator in this endeavor. May the Lord bless them. I am, of course, responsible for the final text.

P. T. Brannan, S.J
St. Charles Borromeo Seminary
Overbrook, Pennsylvania

PREFACE

Four studies make up this work. The first is the re-working of a conference given in 1945 at the *Centre Universitaire Catholique,* and has never been published. The other three appeared during the war in short books under the supervision of M. F. Perroux: the second and third studies were published in 1942 at the *Presses Universitaires de France* in *Communauté et histoire,* the fourth study was in *Communauté et bien commun,* published in 1944 at the *Librairie de Médicis.*

Taken together, these studies seem to cast light on one another, and while being mutually supportive they seem to shed some light on problems which are constantly current.

No matter what the sophists say, history does teach. Perhaps things would go a little less badly in France and in the world if we had a better understanding of, and listened to history's lessons.

A.-J. Festugière

I

FREEDOM AMONG THE GREEKS

The Greek and Christian notions of freedom are certainly two pillars of western civilization. But in what sense is this true?

Freedom, whether word or concept, is not something absolute, but relative. When we speak of a "free man" and wish to analyze this notion, we are immediately led to the contrary idea: "captivity." To be free consists in not being captive, in being "delivered." But from whom or from what is it a deliverance? In the case of Christianity, what we are free of or freed from is most clearly stated in the earliest Christian texts. We are free from sin, from the law of sin. "Jesus then said to the Jews who had believed in him, 'If you continue in my word, you are truly my disciples, and you will know the truth, and the truth will make you free.' They answered him, 'We are descendants of Abraham, and have never been in bondage to anyone *(oudeni dedouleukamen pôpote).* How is it that you say, "You will be made free."' Jesus answered them, 'Truly, truly, I say to you, every one who commits sin is a slave to sin *(doulos estin tês hamartias). . . .* So if the Son makes you free, you will be free indeed'" *(John* 8:31-36). "But thanks be to God, that you who were once slaves of sin *(douloi tês hamartiâs)* have become obedient from the heart to the standard of teaching to which you were committed and, having been set free from sin *(eleutherôthentes apo tês hamartias),* have become slaves of righteousness. . . . But now that you have been set free from sin and have become a slave of God the return you get is sanctification and its end, eternal life" *(Rom.* 6:17-18, 22).[1] St. Paul is permeated with this important theme, we have only to read him to share the sentiments he experienced at the thought that Christ has finally freed mankind from spiritual death. This is the constant teaching of the Church. Consider, for example, the prayer for the feast of Saint Felix of Valois, on November 20th: *Deus, qui beatum Felicem. . . ad munus redimendi captivos caelitus vocare dignatus es*, praesta, quaesumus, ut per gratiam tuam *ex peccatorum nostrorum captivitate eius intercessione liberati, ad caelestem patriam perducamur.*" ("God, who by your divine inspiration vouchsafed to call blessed Felix to the service of redeeming captives, grant, we pray, that through his intercession we may by your grace **be freed from the bondage of our sins** and be lead to our heavenly homeland.")

We see at once where Christian freedom is situated. It is on a moral and spiritual plane, which implies a radical dualism. This level is certainly not wanting in Greek thought. Plato's equally radical dualism of body and soul is proof enough: the soul ensnared in the bonds of the body (*Phaedo,* 83 e 2), fastened as if by a nail to the body (*Phaedo,* 83 d 4), the notion of death as a liberator. Indeed, the theme of deliverance completely pervades the *Phaedo.* (it is philosophy that frees, [*Phaedo*, 82 d 5]) and has made it one of the breviaries of ancient piety. Nor need we dwell on the influence which this Platonic current has exercised on all Hellenistic philosophy.

Nevertheless, when the word and idea of freedom occur in Greek literature, their primary reference is not to spiritual life. Political life is their domain and the expression "Greek freedom" still has political connotations for us. But, we shall see that this concept of freedom among the Greeks, although political in origin, has had the greatest consequences for the very idea of man, for the notion of wisdom with all the nobility, dignity and autonomy it implies among the ancients; that this Greek concept of freedom has consequently strongly influenced the genesis of moral concepts in the West; that it has greatly contributed to the constitution of what may be called "western man," who is, at least in my opinion, "civilized man." For these reasons there is intense interest in analysis of freedom among the Greeks.

This study will entail three parts. First, I shall show how the notion of freedom was formed at the same time as the notion of the city (*polis*) which thoroughly dominated classical Greece. I shall also show how, out of pride in their freedom in the city and a passionate desire to preserve this great good, the citizens of the fifth-century Greek states fought with might and main for the liberty of their fatherland which is identical with their own freedom.

Then, after recalling all that the leaven of freedom caused to burst forth in fifth-century Greece, in a wide variety of human disciplines, I shall indicate how the philosophers of the fourth-century, Plato and Aristotle, defined and specified the notion of freedom in relation to a specific political regime; how they presented at once its advantages and dangers. The advantages were well known at the time and are scarcely mentioned; the dangers seemed formidable and induced them to curtail, rather than to exalt the notion of freedom.

Finally, I shall show the last avatar of this Greek freedom from the time when the fall of the *polis* and the establishment of the monarchy of the Diadochi forced it to seek some sort of refuge in the interior of man. We can be stripped of all things, save freedom of soul. We can be stripped of all things, save of the indefeasible right which we preserve of calling *white* what is white, *unjust* what is unjust, and of developing for ourselves a philosophy of life which satisfies our aspirations. This spectacle of a purely philosophical liberty is apparent even today in an enslaved Greece and it is not the least witness to her greatness.

NOTE

1. In my opinion we must punctuate *to de telos, zôên aiônion*. Free from sin, slave of God, the Christian is already in possession of eternal life. The usual translation is: "and the end is eternal life," with the two accusatives no longer dependent upon *echete,* but on an understood *einai.* This is possible but much more clumsy. And one would expect *zôê aiônios,* as expressed above, *to gar telos. . .thanatos.*

A. POLITICAL FREEDOM

In Greece, the notion of liberty is directly connected with that of democracy *(dêmokratia),* that is to say with the government of the people by the people *(dêmos):* "The foundation of the democratic regime is liberty," says Aristotle *(Pol.,* VI, 2, 1317 a 40) following Plato *(Rep.,* VIII, 557 b 3, 502 b 6). We must consider a bit more closely what the Greeks understood by such an alliance. For us, as for Plato who saw the excesses of this regime during the Peloponnesian War, the word democracy immediately summons up the idea of license. But the fact remains that at the beginnings of the Greek city, it signified a noble human conquest. At the time of Homer (8th c.) and Hesiod (7th c.) the people were of no significance. In the *Iliad,* only the king and the tribal chiefs *(gerontes),* had the right, at the meetings of the assembly *(agora),* to take the scepter and give advice, and to pass sentence. Similarly, in *The Works and the Days,* we see a radical difference between the great land owners who called themselves the people of means and the mass of the little people who toiled rigorously either as veritable slaves, (i.e. serfs), or hired laborers *(thêtes),* or in the completely unstable condition of farmers bound to give up five-sixths of their harvest and allowed to keep only one-sixth *(hektêmoroi)* or of the small free peasants who cultivated only a poor patch. This was a very unstable situation; for, despite the privations which they imposed upon themselves, neither the farmer nor the free peasant could usually make ends meet: the farmer could not pay his rent; the peasant was obliged to borrow. The rich, however, lent with usury and these were difficult times for the debtor. Insolvent, he, his wife and his children were sold into slavery; his field was added to the domain of the rich. As a result, only the rich had true freedom. If the poor wished to gain freedom, freedom in the strict sense, if they wished *to be free in their persons, in their bodies,* they had to group together, they had to unite, in order to compensate by their number for the state of inferiority in which their birth and poverty placed them as individuals.

We need not review here how, as a result of colonization, of the growth of the population in the cities and in the ports, of the increase in commerce and technology, an urban *dêmos* came into being in the seventh century, a *dêmos* more compact and better organized than that of the countryside. This *dêmos* was able to provide itself with leaders to fight against the Eupatrids and finally to force upon them a sort of division of powers. From this compromise came the democratic *polis* in which the genius of Greece is so marvelously expressed.

This change was effected about the year 600. We still possess the text of what is without doubt the most ancient of western constitutional laws. [1] Like the laws of Solon, it was engraved upon a rock cube set upon a stake. This made it possible to turn the stone and read its four faces while remaining in the same place (cf. the *Kyrbeis* of Solon). The text, engraved about the year 600, is quite damaged. But the democratic tenor of the law cannot be denied: the people themselves, the *dêmos,* issue a constitutional law *(rhêtrê)* their demarchs, that is to say magistrates whom they have elected, play a leading role in the government of the city; beside the demarchs appear "kings" *(basileis).* They are a survival of a purely aristocratic or monarchical regime. By general agreement, they come together on certain days in an assembly of the people *(dêmou keklêmenou)* to administer justice. A condemned person can appeal to a council of the people *(dêmosiê boulê),* an elected body composed of fifty members of each tribe which will meet in plenary session on the ninth of each month to administer all the affairs of the people and, in particular, to pass jusgment on all the lawsuits presented during the month (lines, 19-22). At about the same time (592), the laws of Solon assured the Athenians civil liberty for the entire duration of their history by forbidding the seizure of the person of insolvent debtors. [2] All the sons of the Athenians are free citizens, divided into four property classes. Their rights and duties are proportionate to their property, but even the citizens of the lowest class participate in public affairs as members of the Assembly and of the courts. The development thus begun will reach its consummation only with the laws of Pericles in 451 when this statesman will institute payment for public service, a fact which will permit the poorest citizens to have access in practice to all offices, with the sole exception of general *(stratêgos),* because of the capabilities which it demanded.

Thus, the alliance between "freedom" and "democracy" evidently implies two privileges: it implies civil liberty in the sense that every member of the city, born of citizen parents, is secure in his person and in his goods as long as he does not infringe upon any of the civil or political laws of the State; it also implies *political liberty* in the sense that the same citizen, by the very fact of his birth and on the obvious condition of obedience to the laws, is qualified to assume all public offices, whether bestowed by lot or by election. Such a regime is distinct from the oligarchic or aristocratic regime in which power is only in the hands of the small class of the rich or of the best (in the social sense), and it is also distinct from a monarchical or tyrannical regime in which power is only in the hands of a single man whose sole decree establishes law.

A brief response to the earlier question is in order: "What is the object the Greek is free of, that is to say from which he is freed? What is the captivity from which he is delivered?" On the one hand, the Greek is delivered in his very person from the bonds of slavery which actually restrained him (under the guise of serfdom) and which constantly threatened to restrain him, because of the precariousness of his material condition (slavery for debt). On the other hand, he is delivered, precisely as a political animal, from the tyrannical domination of the first masters of Greece, the kings or the feudal lords who owned the land. Such is the original meaning of freedom among the Greeks. [3]

If the merits or defects of a regime are judged by the degree of justice established among men, there can be no doubt that the initial stage of Greek democracy was infinitely better than the purely egoistic oligarchy which it replaced. Let us consider the exact nature of the freedom it conferred.

Aristotle recalls that the foundation of democracy is freedom, that this form of government -- according to common opinion (at Athens) -- is the only one in which men partake of freedom, and that such is the very goal toward which every democratic constitution aims. He then continues as follows (*Pol.*, VI, 1, 1317 b 2): "Now freedom consists, on the one hand, in the fact of being now subject, now ruler *(to en merei archesthai kai archein)* -- for the popular notion of justice is equal rights for all numerically speaking and not according to worth. If such is the notion of justice, the mob necessarily rules: in the final analysis the decision of the majority counts and is law. . . .On the other hand, freedom consists in the fact that each person is free to live as he wills *(to zên hôs bouletai tis):* such is actually the proper function of freedom, if it is true that the characteristic of the slave is not to live as he wills. This then is the second distinctive mark of democracy. From it arises the claim to have no masters: if possible, none at all; if that is impossible, to be now master, now subject. In this way, we tend to achieve freedom in equality for all."

Texts from the fifth century will illustrate this definition, the product of the most lucid and impartial political author of antiquity.

Herodotus suddenly interrupts his account of the conspiracy of Darius against the Persian magi to report that after the murder of the false Smerdis, the seven conspirators got together and three of them -- Otanes, Megabyzus, and Darius -- supported in turn the popular form of government, oligarchy and monarchy respectively (III, 80-82). Clearly, as the most recent editor remarks, [4] these three speeches have no historic verisimilitude; the historian was simply inspired at this point by the sophistic debates which were quite fashionable in Periclean Athens. [5] What, then, in the eyes of Otanes-Herodotus, is the principle advantage of democracy? He has just shown the disadvantages of the monarchical form of government. Entrusting all power to one man who need render account to no one *(mounarchiêi, têi exesti aneuthenôi poieein ta bouletai),* [6] necessarily fills even an excellent man with arrogant insolence *(hybris)* and envy.

Thereafter, the monarch will become a tyrant. He will be incapable of enduring an equal, jealous of his betters, suspicious of flatterers. As one who believes everything is permissable, he will overthrow the most sacred customs and will commit every crime. "On the contrary, the government of the people *(plêthos archon)* has, first of all, the most beautiful of all names: *isonomia* (equality of rights) Second, it does not act at all like a monarch. Its public offices are assigned by lot and each office holder is accountable *(hypeuthynon de archên echei).* All deliberations are brought before the public." Thus, Otanes favors popular government: "For everything rests with the majority, *en gar tôi pollôi eni ta panta."* This passage reveals many features and even expressions dear to the Greek heart in the fifth century. Right off, there is "The most beautiful of all names: *isonomy." Isonomia* is an equal sharing among all; we would say *equality of* civil and political *rights.* [7] To show how familiar this concept and expression were to the fifth-century mind, one example will suffice. Alcmaeon of Crotona, a doctor, wanted to determine the general causes of health and sickness in the light of the medical practices of his day. There were essentially two theories in ancient medicine: one, which may be called the "Dietetic," a patient's good or bad condition depended upon his diet and, in general, upon his whole way of life (physical exercise, rest, etc.); the other, which may be called the "Somatic," made his condition depend upon the good or bad mixture within the body of the four elements or, more precisely, of their fundamental qualities: cold, hot, dry, and moist. Alcmaeon shared this second view which was, in general, that of the medical schools of Sicily and Magna Graecia. Thus he wanted to explain that health depended upon the balance of fundamental qualities. This is how he expressed this position: "*Isonomia* of the qualities, moist and dry, cold and hot, bitter, sweet, etc. maintains health; on the contrary, *monarchia* of one of these is the cause of sickness. For the absolute sway *(monarchia)* of one of the contraries leads to the ruin of the patient. Actually sicknesses arise, as far as their causes are concerned, from the excess of heat or cold. . . . On the other hand, health consists in the well proportioned mixture *(symmetron krasin)* of the qualities" (fr. 4 DK).

Let us now turn to the Peloponnesian War and Pericles' famous oration for the Athenian dead who perished in the first year of this war *(Thuc.,* II, 35 ff.). [8] Pericles begins with praise of their ancestors who "by their military prowess *(di' aretên)* have passed on to their posterity the soil of a fatherland free even to this day (II, 36)." He continues with praise for democracy where we already discover the two distinctive characteristics pointed out by Aristotle: on the one hand, equality of rights *(to ison)* and, on the other, the freedom of each to live as he wishes. He says: "Our constitution is called a democracy, because it is interested not in a small number of individuals, but in the majority. In private disputes all enjoy equal rights before the law; as for honor, no matter what his other merits, each person is usually evaluated for public office on the basis of ability not affiliations. No one seems to have been excluded because of poverty, if he were capable of rendering some service to the State.

These principles of democracy are freely used *(eleutherôs)* in the administration of public affairs and to settle differences in the commerce of daily life. We are not angry if our fellowman acts according to his own will. We no longer inflict punishments which, although they involve no forfeitures, are not less painful to endure before the public eye. Despite ease in private relationships, respectful fear, more than anything else, keeps us from breaking the law in public activity. For we obey not only the successive magistrates in office, but the laws as well, and especially those laws which, though unwritten bring upon the transgressor a universally recognized shame."

This, then, is the ideal of democracy and of freedom. [9] Before pointing out the excesses, we should show how at Athens this principle of freedom gave rise to a prodigious advance of life and of activity in all the human disciplines.

First, without doubt it was the freedom which the Athenians were enjoying as citizens that inspired them to defend themselves unflaggingly against the Persians at the beginning of the fifth century, and against Sparta and her allies at the end of the same century. Tragic poets and historians of the time commonly compare the Greeks to the subjects of the Great King as free men to slaves. They were fighting not only *pro aris et focis,* but also for an ideal life which they had won with great struggle and were certain could alone assure the full development of the human person. In the *Persians* of Aeschylus (472), Atossa asks the chorus (230 ff.): "Where is Athens, is it such a big city, is it so powerful because of its army and treasures that Xerxes thinks he must destroy it? Who, then, are these Athenians, who is their chief in battle, and who governs them as master?" The old men reply: "They call themselves slaves of no man, they obey no one" (242). To be the slave of no man -- that was precisely the Greek's glory. When the Otanes of Herodotus, who expresses the Greek ideal, although he's a Persian, sees his proposal of a democratic regime rejected and monarchy accepted, he says that he refuses, as far as he is concerned, to rule; "but on condition," he adds, "that neither I nor any of my descendents will be subject to any of you" (III, 83). And the historian concludes (III, 84): "Even to this day, the house of Otanes is the only Persian house which is free *(mounê eleutherê)."* In what does this freedom consist? "This house is subject *(archetai)* only in as far as it wishes the king well by transgressing none of the Persian laws *(nomous ouch hyperbainousa)."* This point sums up the precise difference. The Greek obeys no man, but he does obey the law, because the latter is the expression of the will of the people and he is the people. For he is the one who in the council and the assembly has prepared and made the law, and he again is the one who enforces it in the different city tribunals. This political conception is not confined to any particular Greek state. Undoubtedly Athens was its model *(Thuc.,* II, 37), but it had no exclusive claim to it. Herodotus also attributes it to the Spartans in a memorable situation. As he was about to invade the Greek mainland, Xerxes counted his army and his fleet at Doriskos in Thrace (VII, 100). Dazzled by such power, he summoned Demaratus -- the old king of Sparta had been banished from his fatherland and had taken refuge at the Persian court -- and asked him the following question: "How will the Greeks ever be able to resist such a formidable army?" (VII, 101). Demaratus replied that although the Lacedaemonians might have only a thousand men to put in the battle line, they would fight to the last man rather than see Greece enslaved (VII, 102). Xerxes laughed. What will a thousand or five thousand or even fifty thousand do against him? And what is more, men who are equally free and not at all obedient to a single leader! If, on the other hand, the Greeks were governed by a monarch, as the Persians were, they would fear him and out of fear would resign themselves to an unequal combat. But since they are free, they will not fight (VII, 103). And what was Demaratus' reply? "Certainly the Lacedaemonians are free, but they are not absolutely free. They have the law as their master, and they fear it much more than the Persians fear Xerxes. They always do what the law commands. But the precept of the law is always the same: not to flee from combat, however numerous the adversary, to stand firm and to conquer or die" (VII, 103). Athens' resistance in the extremely tragic last years of the Peloponnesian War is clear from the noble passage from *Thucydides* which still condemns Athenian politics after the death of Pericles (II, 65). "Despite their disaster in Sicily, the loss of their entire army and the greater part of their fleet, and although in the city itself there was no longer anything but factions, nonetheless, for three years the Athenians resisted both their ancient enemies and the Sicilians who joined them, and their own allies who for the most part had defected, and finally Cyrus, the son of the Great King, who joined forces with the coalition and supplied the Peloponnesians with money for their navy. In the end, of course, they submitted, but not before their self-defeat at the hands of their own factions."

In the *Persians,* the chorus of old men laments the destruction of the Great King's power. No one will any longer obey the laws of the Empire. No one will any longer pay tribute. No one will any longer fall on his knees to receive the royal commands. The Basileus' (King's) authority is no more (584-590). Then the chorus adds: "Alas there will no longer be any gag for even the tongue. For a people set free speaks freely *(lelutai. . . eleuthera bazein),* once the yoke of authority is removed (594-595)." [10] Obviously, a natural development has taken place from the political meaning of freedom -- the first meaning by the very fact that all freedom is derived from the inalienable right which each person has of using his own person according to his own lights -- to freedom in thought, language, attitudes and conduct. The *eleutheros* ought to behave like a free man. The very adjective *eleutheros*, and still more *eleutherios*, which is derived from it, signify this enrichment of meaning. It would be interesting, but beyond the scope of this study to pursue this semantic evolution. [12] But some examples will illustrate how this spirit of freedom encouraged the spirit of research and discovery among the fifth-century Greeks, just as it encouraged a greater development of personality.

Attic tragedy, the principal major art of the era, is a case in point. An early play of Aeschylus, the *Suppliants*, [No longer deemed necessarily the earliest, but certainly archaic in form. (Trans.)] is hardly yet a drama with living and affective characters. It might rather be compared to an oratorio. How much more vigor is already obvious in the *Persians* (472), although here also the characters function more as symbols than expressions of concrete individual traits. The same can be said for the figure of Eteocles, grandiose as it may be: in the *Seven*, Eteocles **is** resistance and he affects us as such, not because of particular traits which characterize him as an individual. Sophocles is the man who may be said to have freed the personality of the tragic heroes. His first success dates from 468. Ajax, Oedipus, Antigone, Tecmesse, Deianira, and Philoctetes, are interesting as individuals. This liberation was also paralleled by technical innovations. Sophocles introduced the third actor, increased the number of chorus members from twelve to fifteen, broke away from the rule which required the three plays of the trilogy to be associated with the same legend. About this time, Agatharchos discovered the art of perspective and this technical advance was quickly used in theatre scenery. But what really shows the curiosity, the ever fresh ardor of these Greeks, is the fact that in his *Oresteia* (458), the old Aeschylus adopted the innovations of his rival: Agamemnon, Clytemnestra, Cassandra, Electra, Orestes are characters of unforgettable power and vitality.

The art of sculpture -- the classical age begins with the Persian Wars -- reveals an analogous liberation. "Before 500," writes Charles Picard, "there had already appeared some very famous artists, but for the most part there were still *studios*, if not 'schools.' The classicism of the two great centuries of Greece allowed the most expressive triumphs of individualism." [13] To illustrate the progress of sculpture from the time of the Marathonomachs to Phidias, Picard shows a reclining or wounded figure from a pediment of the Delphic Treasury, dating from about 490-484, after the statues of the pediments of the Parthenon. [14]

The art of music reveals similar changes. They are of two types. At the time of Pindar, and surely for some time before, the Greeks were familiar with three musical scales (the enharmonic, the chromatic and the diatonic) which are based respectively on quarter-tones, half-tones and eight tones to the octave without chromatic deviation. The enharmonic scale, of which we can scarcely even form an idea today, afforded only an austere, solemn melody which was fairly monotonous and without appreciable inflexions, without impassioned modulations. [15] It corresponded to the nobility and purity of line of the Dorian style. It was the music that suited sacred poetry, as well as the great Pindaric odes and tragic choruses. It was consonant with the role of moral counsellor which the poets of choral lyric and the tragic choruses in turn were pleased to assume. From the time of Phrynikos (around 500), it was also the only scale accepted for the music which accompanied these choruses. The chromatic, on the other hand, lent itself to appreciable and impassioned melody, to what Plato calls "sugared music" and condemns. [16] For an ancient, the passage from the enharmonic to the chromatic was almost equivalent to the passage from Bach to Schumann for a modern. However, from the time of Euripides, certain musicians attempted to temper the austerity of the enharmonic in the chorus by reconciling its intervals with the half-tone, that is to say by making it completely akin to the chromatic. [17] The final step was taken by the tragic poet Agathon. In 410, he introduced the use of the chromatic to accompany tragic choruses.

The second liberation was a follows. At the time of Pindar, singing voices (in unison!), accompanying music and choreography still formed a close-knit unit in the choral lyric. [18] The music was quite simple: the same melody was repeated in each of the strophes and antistrophes and was varied only in the epode. The music was clearly secondary; voices dominated. Besides, the poet himself composed the music just as he did the words, and he also personally directed the dancing of the chorus. Thus, it was the poet who indeed triumphed: we do not even know the names of the professional instrumentalists, flautists or citharists, who accompanied the performance of the Pindaric odes. But music soon moved beyond this subordinate role. As early as the time of Aeschylus, his rival Pratinus protests, in a hyporcheme, against the liberties taken by the flautists who, by profession, were supposed to accompany the choral chant: "they are not the accompaniment," he says, "the chant of the chorus has become an accompaniment for the playing of the flutes." [19] Towards the middle of the century, music had become sufficiently independent -- of course, it continued to be essentially vocal ensemble -- and the first concert hall was built in Athens, the Odeon of Pericles. Later, under the influence of Timotheus, a friend of Euripides and Philoxenes, music almost became a completely autonomous art and the Athenians loved it. About the same time, the chorus, at least in the comedies, tended to give way to **pure** interludes of music and dance. This already seems to be the case in the *Ecclesiazusae* (392?) and the *Plutus* (388) of Aristophanes. [20] In the comedies of Menander, the chorus has disappeared and is replaced by dances or pantomimes accompanied by music.

The same progress could be shown in still other areas. In prose for example, a development occurs in a few years from the Gorgian period frozen in antithetical structure (every member of the phrase, whether great or small, is rigorously symmetrical) to the infinitely flexible style of the first dialogues of Plato which create the impression of the actual speech of proper Athenian society. [21] Finally, there is an example of medicine. Clerical medicine will triumph in the establishment of the cult of the "miracles" of Asclepius, but, in the last years of the fifth century, we also see the earliest foundations of a lay medicine independent of all superstition and founded solely on experience and reason. As early as the end of the fifth century, it will find expression in the declaration by the author of the *Sacred Sickness* (ch. 1). "This malady does no seem to have any more of the divine about it than the others, nor any more of the sacred, but just as all the other maladies have a natural origin from which they spring, so this malady also has a natural origin and chance cause."

NOTES

1. *Rhêtrê* of Chios. Cf. Tod, *Greek Historical Inscriptions*, 1. Today the stone is fitted into the retaining wall of the modern road which leads south from Chios. For other contemporary texts, see my *Religion grecque* in *l'Histoire Génerale des Religions* (Quillet, 1944), 89-90.

2. Cf. the verses of Solon which Aristotle cites in the Constitution of Athens, XII, 4: *tous d'enthad' autou douliên aeikea/echontas, êthê despotôn tromeumenous/eleutherous ethêka* (The others who endured shameful slavery in their own country and trembled at their masters' moods I have set free.) -- and Plato, *Republic*, VIII, 552 d 9: "Well, then, don't you see beggars in oligarchic states? -- Practically everyone, except the rulers, is such."

3. The term opposed to eleutheros in this first sense is always doulos, which is understood in its original meaning of a slave totally dependent on his master *(despotês)*. Cf. Xenophon, *Cyropaedeia*, VIII, 1, 4: the slave obeys his master *akôn* (unwillingly), the free man *hekôn* (willingly) does praiseworthy deeds.

4. Ph. E. Legrand, *Hérodote* (coll. Budé), III, 106 ff.

5. Herodotus did not leave Athens until 443, and even in Thurii he could keep up with Athenian intellectual and literary fashions.

6. Atossa says the same about her son Xerxes in Aeschylus' *Persae*, 213: "If he fails he is in no way accountable to the country *(ouch hypeuthynos polei)* and, provided he returns, he will always remain master of this land *(têsde koiranei chthonos)*." This word *aneuthynos* as well as *hypeuthynos*, found later in Herodotus, immediately brings to mind Athens. Cf. W. Nestle, *Philologus*, LXX (1911) 252 ff., who rightly sees in these features the influence of Greek sophistic philosophy. On Herodotus' contacts with the sophists, see *ibid.*, 258-265.

7. The number of proper names formed from the adjective is noteworthy, especially if we recall that the choice of prefix in Greek proper names is not unimportant, but aimed at providing a meaning favorable to its bearer. Well, then for Athens alone, according to Kirchner's *Prosopographia Attica* we have: Isagoras (Clisthenes' rival at the end of the sixth century; and with the same formation: Isêgoros), Isarchos *(archon,* 424/3);, Isodêmos (fifth century: Lysias, *pros Isodêmon)*, Isodikê (fifth century: wife of Cimon, son of Miltiades), Isokratês (fifth century: Lysias, *pros Isokratên*), Isolochos (426/5), Isonomos (415), Isotimidês (415) Isotimos (349/8), Isophilos (227/6)

8. Of course, we must recall the role that convention played in the funeral-oration genre which Plato skillfully imitated in his *Menexenus*. The praise of democracy was one of its required parts; cf. *Menex.*, 239 a 1 ff.: "All of us citizens are brothers, born of the same mother (the very land of Attica), and we do not consider ourselves either slaves, or master to one another, but equality of birth *(isogonia)*, set up by nature, obliges us to seek **political equality** *(isonomian)*, set up by law, and to acknowledge no superiority to one another except in the reputation for virtue or wisdom." (In the same dialogue we find again

the theme of free Greeks fighting against the Persians for the freedom of their father land, 239 a 6 ff.)." But, even if it is true that Plato is making fun of these displays which, as he saw it, mistakenly flattered the Athenians, nevertheless it was a fact, and Pericles was perfectly right in recalling it to his audience.

9. It is quite an ideal, and it is as such that Thucydides has Pericles deliver this encomium. On Thucydides' admiration for this statesman (cf. II, 65) where on the occasion of Pericles' death the historian praises his administration of Athenian affairs, and still recognizes that "at the time the government was a democracy only in name, but in fact a monarchy in the hands of its first citizen" *(egigneto te logôi men dêmokratia, ergôi de hypo tou prôtou andros archê)*.

10. On freedom of speech *(parrêsia)* cf. Democritus, fr. 226 DK: *oikêion eleutheriês parrêsie* (freedom of speech is proper to freedom) and the expression of Euripides' *Ion* cited below (note 22 of chapter 3).

11. This point has been brought out well by H. Gomperz, *Die Lebensauffassung der griechischen Philosophen und das Ideal der inneren Freiheit* (Iena-Leipzig, 1904, 34-35). According to this author, the establishment of democracy resulted in the assurance for every citizen of a feeling of freedom which until then had been the nobles' privilege. At the same time it committed the citizens to "noble" or generous feelings: "As a free man the Greek consciously contrasted himself with the slave. As free, he was independent of fate, he had less fears and hopes; he could securely enjoy his own possessions, and he recognized no master over himself except the gods. . . . Consequently it was a sign of a servile soul to appear dependent on fate, or anxious about material success, and a sign of a free-man's soul to appear superior to these material cares and interests. Similarly we find that stinginess in money matters offends the "*bon-ton*," because it was once the sign of belonging to a lower class. But what we indict as a mercenary spirit was viewed by the Greeks as servile behavior. . . . However, to the degree that the philosophers who came from the people considered this type of free man as the universal ideal of man, the ideal of interior liberty took birth in Greek ethics. . . . Whoever measures up to this ideal's demands is a free man; whoever falls short is a slave, even if one sits on a royal throne and the other is sold as a slave in the market. . . . The final justification for these metaphors is the fact that all dependence, all pettiness were perceived as proper to a servile state; all independence, all magnificence as proper to the state of a free man."

12. The same can be said about the substantive *eleutheriotês* : liberality (formed from *eleuthrios*: befitting a free man). A single observation: if Plato, *Rep.* III, 402 c 2, still uses the word in its fuller sense (beside *andreia* : fortitude, *sôphrosynê* : prudence, *megaloprepeia* : magnificence) of "a virtue proper to the *eleutheros* (the free man)" he already limits it to the sense of

"liberality" in money matters in *Theaet.*, 144 d 3. This is a restrictive usage and the only one found in Aristotle *Eth Nic* IV, 1, 1119 b 22 ff. Note, however, that in *Theaet.*, *loc. cit.* Plato modifies the word specifically: *hê tôn chrêmatôn eleutheriotês* (liberality with money) just as Xenophon does in *Symp.* IV, 15: *eleutherios eis chrêmata* liberal in regard to money) while Aristotle uses the adjective and substantive absolutely in this restrictive meaning.

13. *Manuel d' archéologie grecque, La sculpture,* Vol. II, fasc. 1 (1939) 1-2.

14. *Op. cit.,* 522.

15. Certain melodies in plain chant can, in a pinch, approximate it.

16. *hê glykeia mousa* (sweet music), Plato, *Laws,* VII, 802 c 6; Aristoxenus, *Harmonica,* 23, Marquard: *to boulesthai glykainein aei* (the desire to always produce an effect of sweetness). See also Plato, *Symposium,* 187 d-e, *Republic,* X, 607 a: *hê hêdysmenê mousa* (the honeyed muse) and for the condemnation of all novelty in music, IV, 424 c: "the modes of music cannot be changed without overthrowing the fundamental laws of the State," with a reference to Damon (fr. 10, Diels-Kranz).

17. Cf. E. Frank, *Plato und die sogenannten Pythagoreer,* Halle, 1923, 6. See also the protestations of Music in Pherecratus, in Plutarch, *De musica* 1140 D.

18. Cf. A. Croiset, *La poésie de Pindare,* Paris, 1880, 71 ff., 86 ff.

19. Cf. fr. 1 Edmonds *(Lyra Graeca, Loeb Classical Library,* III, 50).

20. Cf. G. Murray, *Aristophanes,* Oxford, 1933, 183.

21. When Gorgias first came to Athens in 427 he was an old man. His *logoi* (arguments) then can go back to the third quarter of the century. Plato's first dialogues, the *Ion,* the first *Alcibiades,* the two *Hippias,* the *Protagoras* probably antedate Socrates' death (399) and could have been written between 403 and 400. This would involve at most an interval of 40 or 50 years.

B. A PHILOSOPHICAL CRITIQUE

OF THE CONCEPT OF FREEDOM

The basis for the argumentation in the personification of the laws in the *Crito* is that law is something of an agreement, of a contract, between the civic community (*to koinon tês poleôs* 50 a 8) and the individual. [1] When he has reached maturity and become acquainted with public life and law, the Athenian citizen is perfectly free to pack up his belongings and go settle elsewhere, if this life and these laws do not suit him (51 d 1 ff.). Socrates did nothing of the sort. He continued to remain in Athens and thus indicated that the laws of Athens and the Athenian political regime satisfied him; he committed himself and cannot now violate this agreement by fleeing Attica (52 b - 53 a). Yet this famous passage contains a most astonishing sentence. It states that Socrates owes everything to the laws of the city. The laws have begotten him; for he was born of a legitimate marriage, consecrated by the law. They have fostered and reared him; for they have prescribed that his father have him instructed in *mousikê* (the arts) and gymnastics. Socrates agrees that the laws are good laws. "Well then, since you have been placed in the world and reared and educated by us (50 e 2, cf. 51 c 8) can you first of all maintain that you and all your descendants do not belong to us (*hêmeteros*), that you are not our offspring and **our slave** (*ekgonos kai doulos*)?" This is a very strange expression indeed. The citizen is a free man in the sense that he does not obey any other man. But he is the slave of the law. The city has made him a free man (*eleutheros*) by guaranteeing him those civil and political liberties defined in the previous chapter, but this same city looks upon him as its slave (*doulos*); for he belongs to it completely. And he belongs to it in virtue of a contract. The city proposes laws in the Assembly: every citizen has the right to agree with or to speak against these laws. [2] If he does not oppose them, he is bound by them. This ultimately comes down to saying that the citizen is a slave in the same degree to which he is free. His liberty involves participation in public affairs. When he participates in public affairs, he is the one who makes the laws. When, therefore, he obeys the law, he is doing nothing else than obeying his own decrees, he is obeying himself.

The consequences of such a conception are obvious. First, there is no true freedom without participation in government, [3] and this involves a commitment. The citizen must assume his responsibilities. [4] Moreover, once the law has been passed -- and the citizen has the right and opportunity to oppose its passage -- the citizen is obliged to follow it without reserve. In short, political freedom imposes intellectual and moral discipline. Government of the people and by the people assumes an education which would make all citizens fully aware of their actions.

This is really the entire problem of Greek liberty. In the famous passage from the *Republic* (VIII, 555 b ff.), excessive liberty is said to lead to *anarchia* (anarchy), that is to say to a State where there is no longer any authority and consequently, where all parties are in conflict. Anarchy leads in its turn to tyranny. On this point Plato's theoretical view does not completely correspond with the actual facts of Greek history. But it is quite interesting to see what the Greeks thought about the abuses of freedom and how Plato came to formulate his doctrine of the evolution of constitutions (timocracy --> oligarchy --> democracy --> tyranny).

The tyrannies of the seventh century clearly did not spring from the excesses of democratic regimes; for there were no democracies at that time, only oligarchies. As a matter of fact, the tyrannies of this age did not follow upon, but preceded popular government. But it is true that the tyrannies were established with the help of the people *(dêmos)*. As the people gradually became conscious of their rights and sought to free themselves from the yoke of their landlords, they allied themselves with one of these landlords against the others. the oligarch who had thus become the "protector" of the people soon set himself up as tyrant. [5] Moreover, since these tyrannical governments were of popular origin, they generally remained, at least in the beginning, favorable to the *dêmos* and hostile to the oligarchs. In this sense Aristotle could write *(Pol., V, 8, 1310 b 15, cf. 5, 1305 a 9)*: "Almost all the tyrants began by being the heads of the popular party, who had won the support of the people by attacking the notables": he cites the instance of Panaetius of Leontini (608 B.C.), of Cypselos of Corinth (655 B.C.), of Peisistratus of Athens (561 B.C.). In another place, he says more explicitly (V, 5.

1305 a 21): "All these protectors of the people *(prostatai tou dêmou)* became tyrants only after having gained the confidence of the people and this confidence came to them because they were seen to hate the rich. Thus Peisistratus became tyrant at Athens after he had formed a party against the proprietors of the plain, and Theagenes at Megara (625 B.C.) after he had slaughtered all the large land-owners' livestock which he had captured while it was grazing near a river." It is also true that tyranny is the result of a period of factions *(staseis)* and murders *(phonoi)*. As early as the fifth century, these two characteristics were observed by the first political writers of Greece. [6] Herodotus is a case in point.

In the previously cited discussion between Otanes, Megabyzus and Darius (Her. III 80-82), Megabyzus criticizes government by the people from the oligarchical view-point, of which he has become the champion. He maintains that nothing is more foolish and more insolent than the mob, and it would be madness to degenerate from the *hybris* of a tyrant to one that is much worse, that of an unbridled populace. For the tyrant knows at least what he is doing, but the mob does not know even this. And how could it, since it has received no instruction, since of itself it has no idea of the good and since it leaps like a torrent into affairs without any reflection -- *aneu noou* (III, 81)? This criticism is hardly original. It merely gives expression to the scorn which all oligarchs regularly entertained for the common people. Theognis, at the end of the seventh century, had already said (53 ff.): "Of course, Cyrnus, this city is still a city, but what a difference in its inhabitants! At one time these wretches were unacquainted with either lawcourts or laws. With well-worn goatskins covering their sides, they used to pasture like deer outside the city. And now, son of Polypaüs, they are the 'honest folk' and those who were once esteemed are of no account today." Of greater interest is the account of Darius (III, 82), who supports monarchy. Government by an individual is the best not only in itself, but also because the two other forms of administration inevitably lead to it. Oligarchy necessarily begets violent hostilities among the privileged who comprise it. From these hostilities spring factions *(stasies)*, from these factions, murder *(phonos)*, and these murders result in monarchy. [7] In the government by the people, the old oligarchs, who have become the *kakoi* (wicked men), form a conspiracy against the commonwealth *(hoi gar kakountes ta koina sunkupsantes poieusi)*. And this state of affairs remains such until one man becomes the people's protector. This man becomes the object of popular admiration and is proclaimed monarch. In fact, the people owe their liberty to him: Since, then, thanks to one man we have been made free *(hêmeas eleuth-erôthentas dia hena andra),* it is to a regime of this nature (monarchical) that we should devote all our care."

It has long been noted [8] that this series of events -- "factions, murders, monarchy" [9] -- is already found in Theognis about the end of the seventh century (v. 43 ff.): The "good," says the poet, has never ruined any city. But when the "wicked" *(toisi kakoisin)* begin to *hybrizein,* (commit outrage), to corrupt the *dêmos,* to render unjust judgments that are favorable to the *dêmos* (people), [10] all because they aspire to wealth and power, then the city's peace is at an end. Yes, even if the city seems to be at peace, all is lost from the very day when the "wicked" choose to grow rich at the commonwealth's expense *(dêmosiôi syn kakôi).* For, as a result, factions spring up *(stasies),* blood flows in the city *(kai emphyloi phonoi andrôn),* and the end result is tyranny *(mounarchoi th').* This is an oligarch's view of the origin of the tyrannies of the seventh-century. The good are the people in office. The wicked are the oligarchs who, in order to attain power, begin to favor the *dêmos.* Internal struggles and finally tyranny ensue. Herodotus took up this formula "factions, murders, etc.," but applied it in this instance to the passage from oligarchy to tyranny. He considered the latter as a good, since it puts an end to rivalry among oligarchs. There is no question of strife between the oligarchs and the popular party. Despite this difference, we can believe with Nestle that Herodotus borrowed this touch from Theognis. [11]

The next section specifically alludes to the case of Peisistra-tus. [12] Democracy is established *(dêmou archontos).* The *kakoi* -- in this instance the oligarchs -- conspire against the commonweal *(ta koina).* Those who were formerly enemies when they alone were in power, now join together in firm and secret friendships *(philiai d'ischyrai . . . sunkupsantes).* [13] As a matter of fact, it is known that when the constitution of Solon had hardly been established, the nobles, because they thought that they were not given enough, stirred up trouble which was brought to an end by Peisistratus. Then one man came forward to protect the people *(prostas tis tou dêmou),* was successful, and was proclaimed tyrant.

The picture is, therefore, accurate on the whole. But it clearly does not present the events as Plato will. The tyrant is not the result of the excesses of freedom. He is rather the one who frees the *dêmos.* [14]

Towards the end of Herodotus' life (he died between 430 and 424) during the early days of the Peloponnesian War, we come across a theory on the genesis of tyranny which approximates the Platonic explanation. [15] It is found in a short political treatise; Iamblichus [16] has saved us some fragments. "(12) Tyranny, which is such a great and deadly evil, is caused only by the abandonment of law *(anomia)*. There are some who think -- and erroneously so -- that the establishment of tyranny has a different origin, that men who lose their liberty are not personally responsible for this loss, but have submitted to the compulsion of a tyrant once set in place. This opinion is not correct. (13) For it is madness to believe that a king or a tyrant can arise from any cause other than the abandonment of law and unbridled ambitions *(ex anomias te kai pleonexias)*. As a matter of fact, this state of affairs occurs only when a city is utterly inclined toward evil: for men cannot live without law and justice. Thus, when the people have abandoned these two things, law and justice; then their supervision and protection passes into the hands of a single man. Indeed, how could one man come to power unless the law which defended the interests of the people had not first been discarded? (15) The man who will abolish justice and suppress the common and useful laws of the people, must have a heart of iron; for he stands against the multitude and must snatch law and justice from the masses. (16) Were he a mere being of flesh and blood, and the equal of others, he could not succeed. His monarchical power would rather consist in the re-establishment of the ancestral constitution." [17]

Here tyranny is clearly shown to result from the corruption of democratic freedom. Through excess of freedom, the people come to *anomia*, that is to say, to a state of affairs where the laws are no longer respected. Then another evil also prevails *pleonexia:* the individuals in the city, now unrestrained, give themselves up to the desire for even greater possessions -- a desire innate in each of us. In a word, private interest outweighs the common good, and factions necessarily ensue. Everyone is bent on evil. There is no longer any law or justice. But life is not possible without direction. Therefore, it is absolutely necessary for one man to take over the controls. This man is the tyrant. Hence, tyranny is seen as the inevitable consequence of the excesses of freedom. This conclusion, the opinion of a supporter of oligarchy, already presents Plato's teaching.

Thucydides has admirably described the excesses of freedom in his summary of the events which followed Pericles' death (II, 65) [18]:

"Pericles used to tell the Athenians that if they remained peaceful, if they took care of their fleet, if they refrained from conquests in war, if, finally, they did not expose the city to danger, they would have the upper hand. But the Athenians did directly the opposite. In matters which seemed even foreign to the war, they managed affairs according to their private ambitions and private interests *(kata tas idias philotimias kai idia kerdê),* to the detriment of themselves and their allies. The success of these enterprises brought honor and profit only to private individuals, while failures hurt the State in her war effort. Pericles' successors were rather equal with one another [19] and each aspired to leadership; also, they began to slacken central government according to the good pleasure of the people. Consequently, as happens in great and powerful states, many mistakes were made, among others, the naval expedition to Sicily. The mistake in this case was not so much going to attack the Sicilians as it was the fact that the very people who launched the expedition were occupied only with their own quarrels for the leadership of the people and paid little attention to the necessary provisioning of their forces. Consequently, not only did they neglect expeditionary concerns, they also then began to become involved in domestic struggles in civic affairs." Internal factions, [20] and not external enemies, were the principal cause of the fall of Athens.

The government of the Thirty Tyrants cannot be said to have been the direct result of the abuses of Athenian democracy. This regime was imposed from the outside. At Athens, it represented the party of the collaborators and immediately aroused an active resistance which finally removed it. The excesses of freedom had most deadly consequences for the Athenians, since they caused them to lose the war, but they did not lead them into tyranny. Plato's source of inspiration for his derivation of tyranny for democracy was not his own native land, but may have been that of Dion I, tyrant of Syracuse (405-367), whom he knew personally.

Now to Plato. In the second to the seventh books of the *Republic,* [21] Plato analyzes the organization of the just city. In the eighth and ninth books, he describes for the sake of contrast, unjust constitutions and their individual characters starting with the regime which is least removed from the just city, timocracy, to that which is farthest removed, tyranny (VIII, 545 c -- IX, 576 b). Plato's description takes up again and develops the pattern which Herodotus pointed out in the speech which he put in the mouth of Darius (III, 82): he derives the regimes from one another progressing from bad to worse. Thus the just city's form of government is considered the best, because philosophers are in power (*ton men dê têi aristokratiai homoion dielêlythamen êdê* 544 e 7). The corruption of this **aristocracy** will give birth to **timocracy** where the leaders seek honor (*hê philotimos politeia* 545 b 5; cf. 545 a 2). From timocracy will come **oligarchy** where the leaders seek only riches. From oligarchy will come **democracy** and from the latter finally **tyranny**. The last stages of the evolution are our present concern.

In Plato's view, the origins of democracy correspond to the facts given above: democracy is established when the *dêmos*, which is poor, realizes that the lords owe their riches only to the cowardice of the poor (*kakiai têi spheterai ploutein tous toioutous* 556 d 6). Then the people revolt, triumph over the rich, "who have been delicately reared and are burdened with excess weight" (556 d 4), massacre or banish most of them and share equally *(ex isou)* with those who remain the government and magistracies which, hereafter, will be obtained by lot. (557 a).

This form of government is essentially based on freedom. "First, isn't it true that people are free in such a state and that freedom reigns -- freedom of speech [22] and the freedom to live as one wishes?" [23] This freedom is apparently something admirable. In this regime, everyone adopts whatever way of life suits him. Nothing is more pluralistic than a democratic state. It is a veritable cloak of many colors (557 b-c); it is no longer one constitutional structure, but an emporium of constitutions (*pantopôlion politeiôn* 557 d 8). Even though competent, no one is forced to govern. On the contrary, citizens can aspire to any office or jury, even should the law forbid it. Isn't this a wonderful and pleasant way to live (557 e - 558 a)? Throughout the state, we find only indulgence and broadmindedness. No one questions how a leader may have prepared himself for public administration: he need only call himself a friend of the people to be overwhelmed with honors (558 b-c). In conclusion, this agreeable form of government, democracy, is really anarchy *(politeia anarchos)*, which indifferently bestows equality on equals and unequals alike (558 c 4-6).

Now, how does the passage from democracy to tyranny come about? By the same kind of disorder which brings about the ruin of every form of government: excessive presence of the characteristic good of this form of government. Democracy aims at freedom which is certainly a good. But democracy loves this good with an insatiable love *(aplêstia)* without any concern for anything else (562 b-c). Thus, "When a democratic state, athirst for freedom, finds at its head bad cupbearers, it knows no restraint and becomes drunk with pure freedom. Then, if the rulers are not extremely accommodating and do not give it complete freedom, it arraigns them and punishes them as criminals and oligarchs (562 c-d)." Then the world is turned upside down. Those who obey the magistrates are treated as voluntary slaves, [24] as people lacking character. In private and public life, praise and honor are given only to those rulers who seem to be subjects and to those subjects who seem to be rulers. In short, anarchy *(anarchia)* reigns supreme (562 d-e). The son is the equal of his father, the resident alien *(metic)* the equal of the citizen, the student the equal of his teacher, the ruler the equal of the old man, the slave the equal of the free man, the wife the equal of her husband, and the animal the equal of the human being (562 e - 563 d). In such an atmosphere of suspicion of even the faintest resemblance to slavery, with such an aversion to recognizing any authority *(hina dê mêdamêi mêdeis autois êi despotês)*, we reach the point where neither the written nor unwritten laws continue to be respected (563 d).

This extreme of freedom is precisely what gives rise to the opposite extreme -- slavery. For if every excess, whether in the seasons, plants or bodies generally leads to a violent reaction, this principle is even more true of political regimes (563 e - 564 b).

How does this transition take place? The democratic state is made up of three classes: those who own nothing, the virulent rabble from whom the leaders are chosen who do nearly all the ruling *(to proestos tês dêmokratias* 564 d 9); those who are orderly by nature, the limited class of the wealthy (564 e 6-7); and finally the people, properly speaking, the mass of workers who are strangers to politics and who, once they are united, make up the most numerous and powerful class (565 a 1-3). Fundamentally, this last class is not directly interested in public affairs. They have to be attracted to the assembly and the best way to do so is to promise them wealth. Such is precisely the game of the leaders. They need a decree of the assembly to legalize the despoiling of the rich. To get such a decree, they hold out to the assemblymen bright promises of a share in the possessions of the rich. When the decree is passed, they keep the greater part for themselves and distribute the left-overs to the people (565 a 4-8). Normally, however, the wealthy defend themselves by speaking in the assembly and by every means in their power. San what they might, from this moment on, they are considered revolutionaries: they are accused of plotting against the people and of working for oligarchy. And so, although not originally oligarchs, they really end up as such (565 b-c). Civil war and endless denunciations and lawsuits are inevitable (565 c 6-7).

Then comes the tyrant's hour. The people are looking for a "protector" (*hena tina aei dêmos eiôthen . . . proistasthai heautou* 565 c 9-10). This protector, who never has anything on his lips but the abolition of debt and the apportionment of land, arms himself with absolute power with the help of the people. Afterwards, he drags the rich before the lawcourts, kills them or exiles them (565 e - 566 a). Having created mortal enemies by such measures and because he fears for his life, he demands protection from the people (566 a-b). This is the last straw. The remaining rich can only flee. The protector of the people is now sole master and becomes a thoroughgoing tyrant (566 c-d).

At first, everything seems to go very well for the people. The tyrant is all smiles, he multiplies his promises, remits debts, reapportions land (566 d-e). But how will he keep himself in power once he has rid the people of the oligarchs and to some degree performed his function as "protector"? To have a *raison d'être*, to preserve his control of the people, keep them busy and keep them from forming a conspiracy, he must constantly stir up wars (566 e - 567 b). These tactics soon make him hateful to the people. The tyranny which did not perhaps need to be cruel in the beginning must become so in the long run. Since it has been illegally established, it can brook no criticism. The tyrant must squelch anyone who is brave, highminded, prudent or rich. Now he must surround himself only with a servile court which he scorns, and with a guard which must increase with the growing number of his enemies (567 b - 568 d). He must maintain and pay his guard. First, he will borrow from the sacred treasury. When these funds are depleted, he will inevitably be led to impose even heavier taxes on the people. The people who had called upon the tyrant only to be freed from the oligarchs will fall into much more painful slavery (568 d - 569 b. Should they wish to revolt, they will have come to recognize their mistake. "We have, it seems, come to what everyone calls tyranny, and the people, while wishing, as it is said, to avoid the smoke of slavery in the service of free men, have fallen into the fire of the despotism of slaves and, in exchange for excessive and inordinate freedom, have taken on the livery of the most dire and bitter servitude by making themselves the slaves of slaves (569 b 8 - c 4)." [25]

Despite Aristotle's criticism (*Pol.*, V, 10, 1316 a 1 - b 27), this magnificently penetrating and forceful picture still retains all its validity. Of course, it certainly does not correspond strictly to the actual facts of Greek history. As Aristotle remarks, the excesses of democracy do not necessarily lead to tyranny; they may just as well lead, and even more frequently do, to an oligarchic regime (1316 a 24-25). On the other hand, every revolution in an oligarchic regime does not necessarily lead to democracy; it can change to other forms of government (1316 b 20-21). The Platonic structure thus seems to be more of a mental construct than the result of experience.

With these reservations, we can only admire the insight of Plato, the political philosopher. History affords ample proof that every illegal dictatorship which has come to power under pretext of defending popular interests has ended in the enslavement of the people; that every dictatorship involves a tyrannical police state that grows in cruelty; finally, that such a regime having exhausted public funds is led of necessity to despoil the sacred treasures. But history also proves that such dictatorships generally follow upon periods of social unrest during which authority is neglected, laws are no longer obeyed, and demagogues no longer govern except by illegal decrees. Thus the illegality of the tyrant arises from this fundamental illegality which resulted from the excesses of popular government. Tyranny comes from anarchy. If democracy's greatest good is obviously freedom, freedom, in turn, finds its greatest security only in respect for the laws and common concern for the public interest.

NOTES

1. Cf. 50 C 5: *ô Sôkrates, ê kai tauta hômologêto hêmin te kai soi . . .;* ("Did you and we agree on these terms too, Socrates?"); 51 e 3: *êdê phamen touton hômologêkenai ergôi hêmin ha an hêmeis keleuômen poiêsein tauta,* ("Now we say that man has actually agreed with us -- or promised us -- to do what we may command"); 52 d 2: *para tas synthêkas te kai tas homologias kath' has hêmin synethou politeuesthai,* ("in violation of the contracts and agreements by which you agreed with us to live as a member of the state"); 52 d 4: *phaskontes se hômologêkenai polituesthai kath' hêmas ergôi, all' ou logôi,* ("when we say that you agreed to live as a citizen in conformity with us in deed not in word"); 52 d 9: *allo ti oun ê synthêkas tas pros hêmas autous kai homologias parabaineis,* ("Aren't you transgressing the contract and agreements made

with us?" 53 a 5: *nyn de ouk emmeneis tois hômologêmenois,* ("Well, then, won't you stand by your agreements?").

2. *Peithein* 53 a 3. Literally: "to persuade" the Assembly by a speech to reject this position. That is exactly the job of the public speaker.

3. At Athens this happened without middle-man. There were no delegates on the Assembly and law-courts.

4. If we are to trust Aristotle, *Constitution of Athens,* VIII, 5, Solon would have sentenced those who failed to take up arms for either side in civic discord to the loss of civil rights *(atimia).*

5. *Prostas tis tou dêmou* ("some protector of the popular party") Herodotus, III, 82; cf. Plato, *Republic* VIII 565 d 1: *dêlon hoti, hotanper phyêtai tyrannos, ek prostatikês rizês . . . ekblastanei* ("It is clear that whenever a tyrant springs up he sprouts out of a protector's roots.") Herodotus and Plato have in mind Peisistratus' case which was classic in Athens. Moreover this case differs in part form that of the tyrants of the 7th century. Peisistratus' tyranny came about after the establishment of an early form of democracy by Solon in 592 (Assembly, Council, popular courts).

6. On the political literature of fifth-century Athens cf. Wilamowitz, *Aristoteles und Athen,* I, 169 ff.

7. Aristotle, *Politics,* V, 12, 1316a 35 ff, cites a certain number of cases where oligarchy became tyranny. He says that most of the Ancient Sicilian oligarchies became tyrannies (e.g., at Leontini, Gela, Rhegium).

8. Cf. W. Nestle, *Philologus,* LXX (1911) 253 ff.

9. Theognis and the fifth-century authors still use *monarchia* indifferently for monarchy and tyranny. The distinction dates only to the fourth century. Cf. Wilamowitz, *Aristoteles und Athen,* I, 181, n. 85 and Aristotle, *Politics,* V, 10, 1310 b 1 ff.

10. That is the true meaning of *dikas t'adikoisi didôsin* ("they give judgment to the unjust"). The unjust here are the good people. Cf. the story of Deioces in Herodotus, I, 96 ff.

11. *Philologus, loc. cit.,* 252.

12. Herodotus dwells on this, I, 59 ff.

13. It is possible that Herodotus is here making an allusion to the

formation of the oligarchic clubs in the Athens of his time. It is also possible that this praise of monarchy, of a monarch to whom the people owe their freedom, is more or less inspired by the example of Pericles under whom the democracy was in fact *hypo tou prôtou andros archê* "the rule of the first citizen" (Thucydides, II, 65). In any case the description of the oligarchs as *kakoi* ("evil men") seems to come from a lampoon of anti-oligarchical bent.

14. *eleutherôthentas dia hena andra* (set free by one man). This could apply to Cyrus. Cf. Aristotle, *Politics* V, 8, 1310 b 38: *hoi d'eleutherôsantes hôsper Kyros* ("while others, like Cyrus, set them free"). It, however, applies just as well to Peisistratus.

15. *Anonymus Iamblichi,* Fr. 7, 12ff = Diels-Kranz, *Vorsokatiker,* II, 404, 16 ff.

16. In the *Protrepticus*.

17. The conclusion of the text is not certain.

18. I have made much use of the often-excellent translation of Ambroise Firmin-Didot (Paris, 1833).

19. Pericles alone had been superior to all the others.

20. *en stasei ontes . . . , autoi en sphisi kata tas idias diaphoras peripesontes.* (In civil strife they were caught in their own differences.)

21. Summed up at the beginning of book VIII, 543 a-c.

22. *parrêsia* (Freedom of Speech). Cf. Euripides, *Ion.* 671-672: *ek tôn Athênôn m'ê tekous' eiê gynê / hôs moi genêtai mêtrothen parrêsia.* ("May the one who bore me be an Athenian so that I may have freedom of speech from my mother.")

23. *exousia. . . poiein ho ti tis bouletai* (license to do whatever one wishes) 557 b 5; cf. Thucydides, II 37 and Aristotle, *Politics* VI, 1, 1317 b 12: *to zên hôs bouletai tis* (to live as one wishes).

24. *ethelodoulous* (willing slaves): cf. Tacitus' *ruere in servitutem* (rush into slavery).

25. Modified version of Chambry's translation. These slaves, whose slaves are the people, are the tyrant's paid bodyguards.

C. INTERIOR FREEDOM OF THE
WISE MAN

In 338/337, a few weeks after the battle of Chaeronea, the Greek cities made a treaty of alliance with Philip at Corinth. They swore not to bear arms against Philip, of course, or against any of the cities of the alliance: not to seek the overthrow of Philip's monarchy, or that of his successors, or of the regimes then in power in the cities of the alliance. If one of the cities broke the pact and disturbed the common peace, the others were to make war on it, "in accordance," said the text of the oath, "with what has been enjoined and with the commands of the supreme commander," that is to say, the king of Macedonia. [1] This memorable date not only marks the end of the autonomy of the Greek cities, it also opens a new period in the moral and spiritual life of Western Man.

Up to this time, ancient man, considered as a moral person, was defined essentially as a member of a city. The citizen was by nature an *eleutheros* (free man), in the sense that he obeyed no one else, that he was in no one's service. [2] He obeyed only the law, and the law, as we have seen, is an agreement which the citizen, in theory, has freely contracted with the city. On the other hand, the city was also free. No matter how small -- for the extent of its domain in no way modifies its rights -- it was absolute master of its actions: it decided peace and war, changed its constitution at will, and governed itself in complete independence. From the time of the Corinthian League, the city was no longer autonomous. It obeyed one master, the king of Macedonia. After a few revolts, Athens would be garrisoned with Macedonian soldiers and, in accordance with the sovereign's orders, governed by a particular party.

Even in modern states, such great changes would profoundly disturb the moral conscience. But still modern man finds some refuges: religion, philosophy, the findings of the pure sciences. The inhabitant of classical Greece did not have these means of support. For him, the state was everything. It was a Church, for religion was scarcely distinct from the city. It taught him how to live and offered the citizen the most beautiful goal to which he could give himself: the service of the fatherland. Even Plato, at the Academy, sought to form future rulers. His sole intent was the good of the city. Only the method has changed, not the end. Isocrates did the same thing in his school. We can imagine, then, what the downfall of the city meant to the ancient. His whole world crumbled. Rarely have thinking men been called upon to revise their values and their whole understanding of life so completely.

In analogous circumstances, modern man can take refuge in religion, philosophy, or science, as I have said. However, these three ways of life were set up in complete autonomy at this precise time. In this epoch, under the influence of the *Timaeus*, of the *Laws*, of the *Epinomis*, and of the *peri philosophias* of Aristotle, there is set up the religion of the cosmic deity which at last proposes to man an object of adoration which is capable of satisfying at the same time the demands of his reason and of his heart while simultaneously showing him in the skies and the divine stars an object of contemplation which enraptures him and delivers him from worldly miseries. Isocrates and Plato wanted to form rulers; Aristotle aimed at promoting merely science. The Lyceum is the first establishment of antiquity which could be said to be devoted to pure science. From the Lyceum the tradition will pass to the Museum of Alexandria. The works of the Alexandrian critics will establish the texts of the great works of the past, and prepare for the great discoveries of the future. Finally, at this time philosophy also truly becomes a refuge. Epicurus, in 306, founded the school of the Garden; Zeno, in 301 that of the Stoa. Both of them are going to furnish man with new settings meant to replace that of the vanished city.

In the philosophy of the Garden, the new milieu in which man will feel at home and will develop at his ease, will be the family of his "friends." Epicurean friendship is not only the exterior sign which links together the disciples of the master, but is the very foundation of wisdom. [3]   Man ought to strive for freedom from trouble *(ataraxy)*. But only if he is sustained, comforted, and consoled by the presence and affection of the society of his "friends" can he attain this end. In the philosophy of the Stoa, the concept of the city is extended to the universe. The wise man is a citizen of the city of the world in which the regular movements of the stars manifest an Order and a Thought. One and the same Soul, one and the Reason penetrate all the beings of the world, but they appear especially in man and in the astral deities which are also endowed with reason. The world is, therefore, the true city, if we wish to find the true family in which man is a relative of the gods. Hence, this man is no longer alone. He is no longer alone in the midst of the small groups of friends which the disciples of Epicurus formed. At the same time, he is no longer alone in the city of the world, for he can, at every moment return in thought to his divine family.

Thus the sages of Athens, in this time of profound misery, gave to the world a new conception of freedom. Till then, Athens had always been the champion of freedom: it had championed the individual in the city, and the city in Greece. When political freedom was lost, the philosophers of Athens taught that the Wise man remains free, if he learns to be self-sufficient and to live in accord with the world order. [4] The historian Hegesander phrased it well: "If everything else is common to all the Greeks, Athens alone knew how to show men the way which leads to heaven." [5]

Now, instead of getting lost in fine points of doctrine, let us face reality, life. Let us ask how it happened that these Hellenistic moralities were truly instruments of consolation and strength, how it has come about also that unlike the ethical systems of Plato and Aristotle which no longer have any meaning for us, those of Epicurus and of Zeno still have some followers who are perhaps unaware of their membership in these sects, but who are nonetheless authentic Epicureans (I am using the term in its true sense), authentic Stoics.

Epicurus was sickly. Cleanthes a water carrier who worked at night for a bakeress. Epictetus was a slave, then an exile. Epicurus and Zeno lived in an age in which famine and death were constant dangers.Epicurus founded the Garden in 306, he died in 270. Zeno founded the Stoa in 301, he died in 261. In this space of forty-five years, scarcely a lifetime, Athens changed hands seven times: there were three revolutions which ended in blood; there were five blockades, and the city was captured three times; finally, during these forty-five years, Macedonian garrisons occupied the Piraeus, the ports of Attica, and for five years even the hill of the Muses in Athens. Certainly this was one of those times when one would have a sense of the absurd, when the absurd seemed to govern the world. The notion of the absurd appears for the first time in the philosophy of life, precisely at this time, under the name of *Tyche*, Chance, Fortune. The Hellenistic age makes Fortune a goddess, the sole all-powerful divinity. These two systems of morality were formed, therefore, in times of misery, and they fit in with the misery of modern man who likewise came upon the scene at this time. Modern man, that is to say, man adrift, the inhabitant of big cities, lost in the crowd, a mere cipher in the midst of an infinity of human beings equal to himself, who know nothing about him and about whom he knows nothing. Man who is to bear the burden of life alone, without a confidant, without purpose, without a *raison d'être*,who goes around in circles like a beast, until he dies and that's that.

Epicurus and Zeno, however, have furnished this man with some elementary lessons on the happy life which have value even today. They taught the way to obtain interior freedom. Just what is their secret?

With little reflection, we perceive that there are not many ways to obtain peace of soul. What disturbs this peace is suffering; the cause of suffering is the lack of harmony between our desires and reality. In theory there are three ways to get rid of this lack of harmony: either change reality so that it corresponds to our desires, or get rid of our desires, or to transform them to adjust to reality.

The first way is evidently impossible, at least for man. We cannot change reality. The most that we can do is to put ourselves in such a physical and psychological state by orgiastic dances and drugs, that we imagine reality to be other than it is. Antiquity was familiar with the orgies of Dionysus (Euripides, *Bacchantes*) or of the *Magna Mater*. Modern man is familiar with drugs. Besides other inconveniences, these means produce only transitory effects. Wisdom is completely different from them.

Since we cannot change reality, the only thing left, therefore, is to change or at most suppress desire. But once again it is impossible to change desire completely. A being who no longer has any desire is a being who no longer has any form of life -- a corpse. All we can do is distinguish between desires and satisfy only those which cannot be disregarded without death. What are these irrepressible desires of the living being? "The flesh cries out: do not go hungry, do not go thirsty, do not be cold," Epicurus reminds us. Only those desires which aim at the simple preservation of the living person are retained as necessary and natural. But it is the easiest thing in the world to satisfy these desires. A handful of beans, a little bit of water, a coarse cloak, [6] and your wise man is, says Epicurus, capable of rivaling Zeus himself in happiness.

I have mentioned Epicurus. But this progressive elimination of desires, this wisdom which aims at what we might call "the ideal of the minimum" is common as well to all the Hellenistic schools whose ideal is the independence of the wise man: to the Cynics, the Epicurians, and the Stoics. Moreover, it is found among the fathers of the desert and among innumerable Christian ascetics. Furthermore, it is one of the dogmas of oriental wisdom, and it is not unreasonable to compare Diogenes or Epicurus to Buddha. In brief, although quite ignored today, we have here a tendency that is deeply rooted in the human soul: thousands have endeavored to extinguish, as far as is possible, all their desires in the belief that it would lead to an infinitely more precious good: interior freedom, peace of soul, that state which, according to the expression of the ancients, resembles the perfectly calm surface of the placid sea *(galênismos)*.

But is this all? I have my lupin, my glass of water and my cape. I have suppressed, by hypothesis, every vain desire. Am I happy? Alas, there is still fear: fear of the gods, fear of death, fear of suffering!

The fear of the gods! This might seem strange to the modern man who is no longer a religious animal. But any religious experience is enough to reveal how forcefully and deeply this fear grips the soul. The most basic fact of religion is the feeling of terror, and, as it were, of sacred horror, which we experience from contact with, or even at the mere approach of this radically **other** being which is the Divinity. This fundamental otherness of the divine is, as a matter of fact, inexpressible. We express it only in secondary differences: the sacred, opposed to the profane; the pure, opposed to the impure. We feel that this sacred thing belongs to another world, that it is unattainable, ineffable.

We also perceive that in comparison to this pure absolute we are essentially impure. From this source comes the notion of sin, of defilement, which is common to all religions. All the unhappiness which befalls us, the catastrophes which destroy harvests, bring disease on cattle, make women sterile, plague, famine, war, all these seem to us to be the result of a fault which we have committed and which has vexed the gods. Consequently we live in constant dread of having offended the Divinity.

If on the other hand, we believe in a future life, where we will be happy or unhappy according to our conduct here on earth, our fears embrace not only our present life, but also our lot after death. Consequently it can happen, and it happens every day, that some profoundly religious persons derive from religion nothing but continual anxiety. Religion is a burden for them. And whoever delivers them from this burden will be considered a wise man. Such was Epicurus. His chief merit, in the eyes of many (Lucretius, for example), was to have delivered men from the fear of the gods. But why are the gods not forbidding, according to Epicurus? Because they can have no influence over world events. This is proved in two ways. On the one hand, these events are completely dependent upon material causes: the atoms in motion, and chance which causes the atoms to join unpredictably in an infinite number of ways. Epicurus is a pure materialist. On the other hand, this independence flows from the very nature of the gods. If they exist, they are happy. If they are happy, they have no cares. How then are we to suppose that they are concerned with the government of the world and human affairs? Epicurus' first "Principle Doctrine" is that "The happy and immortal being neither knows trouble nor causes it to another: hence he is susceptible to neither wrath nor fear."

It is a waste of time to fear death. At death we disintegrate. But whatever disintegrates, no longer has sensation.

Suffering either endures and is then tolerable, or is intolerable and does not endure: either it ceases or it kills us.

The Epicurean is therefore free. He no longer has any desires or fears. He is free to be concerned with his soul, to take care of his soul in the company of some friends who, like himself, are taking care of their souls. To live as sheltered as possible from all affairs, to refuse every office, every function, to surround himself with some trusted friends who, as himself, have chosen to devote themselves completely to the healing of the soul, this is the ideal of interior freedom as conceived by Epicureanism. There are still many Epicureans among us.

The last means, as I have said, is to transform our desires. We cannot change the reality which causes us suffering, but suppose we judge this reality good, good by nature, in its very being? Will it not be the part of wisdom then to be in harmony with reality? This is the Stoic solution, and it has had a decisive influence on human thought.

Stoicism, to tell the truth, did not invent it. Plato already formulated it in a famous passage of *The Laws* (X. 903 b-d). We suffer and this suffering appears to us as a disturbance. But this disturbed feeling comes from the fact that we have considered only a part of reality. We do not look at the Whole. If we consider the Whole, it can appear to us only as an order. But where there is order there is unity composed of parts which are necessarily unequal. Being unequal, they are distinguished by different degrees of goodness. None of them is perfect goodness. The only goodness which each has is that which is proper to it, and this can be only the sole fact of existence. But these parts are all needed to make up the complete Order which alone is perfect. Consequently, disorder is absorbed in order. Evil is only a less good and this partial evil is indispensable, if we desire the existence of the Whole. Wisdom, therefore, consists in looking at the Whole (Marcus Aurelius, XII, 18, 2; Plotinus, II, 9, 9, 75).

Interior freedom, therefore, consists in changing our desires, in sublimating them, in transposing them from the individual plane to that of the universe. We desire personal happiness: a vain quest! The happiness of the Whole must be desired. And since the Whole is necessarily good, and therefore happy, it is necessary to rejoice in this good of the Whole, in its perfection and happiness. "To be in harmony with universal nature," such is the only precept of ethics. It is the only one, for it is sufficient. As a matter of fact, once I am in harmony with the universe, I can only act in conformity with this harmony. All particular laws are therefore useless. I possess all wisdom and it is impossible for me to do anything which is not in accord with wisdom. A person is either completely wise or is not wise at all.

But if I am now completely wise, because I am in harmony with the universe, I become free to do as I please, I enjoy complete freedom. I am completely indifferent to the fortunate or unfortunate outcome of my actions. What counts is the form that I give them, and this form excels all others. Thus we arrive at absolute indifference. Everything is good, since everything happens according to the world's law which is good. And I need only blindly follow this law of the world for everything that happens to me, whatever it may be, to appear to me equally good. Life becomes an utter game. Of course I act, because I live. But I act like a child who is playing ball and who is preoccupied only with catching and throwing it well, without any concern for winning the game. I am a good citizen, a good husband, a good father, a good friend. If I see a man fall into the sea, I jump in to save him. If I can be of help, I help. But my only reason for acting thus is to be in conformity with my nature which is itself in harmony with the universal nature, and by no means to fulfill a duty, or perform a good deed, or to achieve a good result. If a man drowns, so much the worse. If my help fails, so much the worse. So much the worse or so much the better; it really doesn't matter. Everything is good. The world is good, and I am in harmony with the world.

We cannot help but compare this attitude with that implied in Augustine's phrase: *Ama et fac quod vis.* "Love God," that is to say, conform yourself with God. Desire all that God desires. Judge good all that God decrees. Aim at what fully realizes God's order. And then, "Do what you will." You possess love -- Christian charity -- and therefore everything you do is good. There is no doubt that the Stoic formula leads to the extreme of interior freedom, and that in discovering this formula, the Stoa has given to the world a powerful potion for peace.

But there is a difference between the attitude of the wise man and that of the Christian. The wise man's attitude completely lacks dynamism. This is evident, if we consider the disciples of Epicurus. But it is no less true in the case of the Stoic. It is of course quite true that the secret of happiness consists in sublimating our desires, in transposing them from the plane of the Ego to the plane of the Whole, of the order of the Whole. But this Order for the Stoic is a purely static Order. It is a datum. It exists once and for all. It is perfect as it is. There is nothing to change in it. We can only accept it as it is. Everything that happens is good. The whole chain of events, the whole progress of Fatality, expresses a perfectly wise and just, a perfectly ordered Necessity. Therefore, I need only submit to it. As soon as I submit, I reach wisdom and freedom.

But fundamentally, why continue to act at all, if my action is going to change nothing in the order of things and if, whether I act of not, everything is equally good? Everything should be as it is, and I need only say "so much the better." Then let us let things be. Let us let the stream of life pass, let us stay on the bank to watch this stream, to contemplate the excellence of the universal Order: let us remain merely passive.

The Christian Order is completely different. This Order is being established. The holy City is being built. Till the end of the world it will be under construction, since all souls, even the last, have been called to take their place in this edifice. From another viewpoint, this City is being built by us, in continuation of the work of Jesus Christ. I am responsible for the salvation of my brothers. The salvation of a particular soul depends upon me, my efforts, my sacrifices and my tears. This is, therefore, an essentially dynamic order and the mere awareness of this fact is sufficient to prevent me from remaining passive. I am an indispensable collaborator with God. My action is necessary for God. If I do not act, a particular soul will not be saved.

Christian love, Christian charity, therefore, has furnished the world with something more than Stoicism. The Stoic sage, on the supposition that one is possible and that one does exist, is certainly free. But he is free only with the liberty of indifference. Why choose this rather than that, since everything is reduced to the same? In the end, this wisdom approaches that of Epicurus: it leads as did his, to a sort of nirvana. The Christian who loves is also free. *Ama et fac quod vis.* But in the very degree to which he loves, this love dictates choices to him. "The Charity of Jesus Christ urges me on," says St. Paul (2 *Cor.* 5:14). Pascal says, "Jesus Christ will be in agony until the end of the world: we must not sleep during this time."

NOTES

1. Dittenberger, *Sylloge inscriptionum graecarum,* 260.

2. The fact of slavery must be admitted; but the precise point is that the slave is not a moral person.

3. On this point, see my book, *Epicure et ses dieux,* Paris, 1946, ch. III. (Tr. by C. W. Chilton: *Epicurus and His Gods,* Cambridge, Mass., 1956).

4. Obviously we must recall with H. Gomperz (*op. cit.,* 92) that this ideal of interior freedom was not unknown to the pre-hellenistic philosophers. The example of Socrates' life and especially of his death played a decisive role in this issue. Cf. his final farewell to his judges, *Apology* , 41 d 1: "No evil can befall a good man either in life or in death, and the gods are not indiffer-

ent to his lot," noble words which are echoed at the conclusion of the *Republic* before the myth of Er, the Pamphylian: "We must admit this about the just man: if he is exposed to poverty, to sickness, or to any other condition which is considered evil, it will turn out for his advantage, either in life or in death. For the gods cannot overlook a man who strives to become just and to make himself, as far as man can, like to god by the practice of virtue." (X, 613 a 5 - b 1). The fact remains, however, that the philosopher of Classical Greece, e.g., Socrates and Plato, sought to reform the earthly city, and aimed at educating men who would manage its affairs according to the Just City's model. The Hellenistic wise man gave up this plan: his thought was only for the individual's salvation.

5. In Athenagoras, VI, 250 f: *talla panta einai koina Hellênôn, tên d'epi ton ouranon anthrôpous pherousan hodon Athênaious eidenai monous.* Hegesander of Delphi lived towards the middle of the 2nd century B.C. Cf. Jacoby, in *Paully-Wissowa*, VII, 2600-2602.

6. The famous *tribôn* (tread-bare cloak) of the philosophers was already with Socrates: Cf. Amipsias, *Konnos*, fr. 1; Plato, *Protagoras* 335 d, *Symposim* 219 b. Cloak, staff, and leather pouch (*tribôn, baktron, pêra*) became the insignia of the wise man (Cynic): cf. Diogenes Laertius, VI, 13 (Antisthenes), 22-23 (Diogenes).

APPENDIX

I am adding some texts and elucidations. They have in common the tendency to find a principle which will make the wise man completely independent: this principle is *autarkeia,* that is, the state in which a person is completely self-sufficient.

EPICURUS [1]

"Complete independence (self-sufficiency) is the greatest of riches" (Fr. 70 *B.* = 476 *U*).

"The most precious fruit of complete independence (self-sufficiency) is freedom" (*G. V.* 77).

"We consider complete independence (self-sufficiency) a great good, not because we always wish to rest content with the minimum, but in order to rest content with this minimum if we cannot have much, in the firm conviction that they most enjoy the luxuries of the table who have the least need of them; that the demands of the natural desires are obtained with ease, those of useless desires with difficulty" (*Ep.,* III, 130, cf. Fr. 29 *B*).

"The study of nature does not lead to vanity, or to verbal dexterity, or to a display of that culture on which men pride themselves; rather it teaches high-spiritedness, complete independence (self-sufficiency), and leads one to pride himself only on those goods which he has in himself and not on those which he owes to circumstances" (*G. V.* 45 [2]).

"The man who obeys nature and not vain opinions is independent (self-sufficient) in all things (*en pasin autarkês*). For as regards what is sufficient for nature, no matter how little a man has, he is rich; while as regards limitless appetites, even the greatest opulence <is not opulence but poverty> (Fr. 45 *B.* = 202 *U.*, cf. *G. V.* 25).

"When the wise man has perfectly adapted himself [3] to the strict minimum necessary for life (*eis ta anankaia*), he is more apt to give of his possessions than to receive from others: so great is this treasure of total independence (self-sufficiency) which he has discovered" (*G>V>*. 44).

"A free life *(eleutheros bios)* cannot acquire many goods because this is not easily done without making oneself the servant of the populace or of monarchs; and, nevertheless, the free life possesses all goods in uninterrupted abundance" (*G>V*. 67).

Finally, there is testimony of one of Epicurus' first disciples, perhaps Hermarchus: "You would think that you were listening to a fable, if Epicurus' life were to be compared to those of others with respect to peace and total independence (self-sufficiency)" (*G>V*. 36).

STOICS [4]

The idea of freedom has a twofold meaning among the Stoics.

On the one hand the wise man is free to the degree in which he, like the universe, [5] is entirely self-sufficient. But he is self-sufficient because he possesses virtue, and because virtue is enough in itself for happiness: "According to Zeno, Chrysippus in the First Book of his work *On Virtues,* and Hecato in the Second Book of his work *On Goods,* virtue is enough in itself for beatitude. For he (Chrysippus) says if magnanimity is sufficient to elevate a soul above all things, but is only a part of virtue, virtue itself is enough in itself for beatitude, since it disregards things which seem misfortunes" (*S>V>F*. I, 187 and III, 49). Consequently the wise man is completely independent. He is independent with respect to the great ones of this world: "Zeno correcting Sophocles' saying (Fr. 253 N) 'The man who goes to a tyrant's house becomes his slave, even if he was free when he arrived,' re-wrote it thus: 'does not become his slave if he was truly free when he arrived.' For he now understood by this word 'free' the fearless man, the magnanimous man who is indomitable" (*S>V>F*. I 219). Nothing can coerce the wise man. As Zeno says: "Sooner would you thrust an air-inflated skin into water than force a wise man, whoever he may be, to do an act contrary to his will despite himself: his soul is inflexible and invincible because right reason has put it in shape [6] with solid doctrines" (*S.V.F.*, I, 218). The wise man is no less independent with respect to fortune's goods: "In the Second Book of his work *On Life Styles,* he (Chrysippus) also deals with the question of 'Whether making money should be a concern,' and he shows how the wise man should behave. Why would the wise man earn a living? In order to live? But life is a matter of indifference. In order to gain pleasure? But pleasure is also an object of indifference. In order to practice virtue? But virtue has within itself all the requirements for happiness. Moreover, all the ways used to make a living are contemptible. Do we turn to a prince? He will have to be given in to. Do we turn to our friends? Then friendship is bartered for profit. Do we make a living out of wisdom? That's trafficking in wisdom?" (*S>V>F>.*, III, 685). In brief, virtue alone furnishes us with everything necessary for life. "*Autarkeia* is an habitual disposition *(hexis)* which is content with the indispensable *(arkoumenê hois dei)* and which of itself furnishes what is necessary for life" (*S>V>F>.*, III, 272). [7]

On the other hand, the wise man is free --and really he is alone in being truly free -- because he obeys the divine Law, that universal Reason in which he himself participates by his own reason. Interiorly he bears the mark of God and, since he is fixed in this conformity, or, in other words, fixed in wisdom, he is free to act as he wills. For he behaves well in all circumstance. Since he is in harmony with the world's Reason, and since this initial agreement gives all his actions their specific character, his actions are necessarily good. Consequently the Stoic wise man, according to a famous paradox, could be called the only real citizen, the only real relative, real friend, and genuine free man. "In his *Republic,* Zeno has shown that only the wise man deserves to be called citizen, friend, relative and free man" (*S>V>F.*, I, 222). "Only the wise man is free, the non-wise are slaves. Actually, freedom is the ability to act as one pleases *(autopragia);* slavery is the privation of this ability" (*S>V>F.*, III, 355). However, we owe this ability to act as we please to our conformity to the divine Law: by reason of this Law itself we have the right to determine our own actions. [8] "All who live in accordance with the Law are free. For the true Law is right judgment which has been engraved in indelible characters in our immortal reason by immortal nature" (*S>V>F.*, III, 360). This is why the wise man alone is free: on the contrary, the non-wise is a slave because of his soul's slavish bent (*S.V.F.*, III, 593).

Many works of the first and second century of our era focus on this idea of the wise man's freedom: Philo's treatise *Every Wise Man Is Free* (Vol. VI, Cohn-Wendland), Plutarch's treatise *On True Nobility (peri eugeneias)*, Dio Chrysostom's discourses *On Slavery and Freedom* (XIV-XV, Vol. II, 64 and 65 Von Arnim), the lengthy chapter *On Freedom* (IV, 1) in Epictetus' *Discourses,* and finally an inscription carved in the rock in a sanctuary of Apollo in Pisidia. [9] It would be quite interesting to compare these works and to show their significance for spiritual life during the Empire. [10] It would also be rather interesting to study the idea of interior freedom in Epictetus. It has been noted that the words *eleutheros, eleutherô, eleutheria,* occur about 130 times in Epictetus. [11] This is six times their frequency in the New Testament, and twice their occurrence in Marcus Aurelius. Epictetus was born a slave and at Rome fell into the service of Epaphroditus, a freedman of Nero, who maltreated him, according to some traditions. After gaining his freedom, he was sent into exile in Nicopolis (Epirus). He knew the nature of slavery from experience and the value of acquiring freedom of soul in such a condition. His experiences explain his insistant treatment of freedom and emphatic conviction of statement.

But I cannot go further. I limit myself finally to a translation of the Pisidian inscription mentioned above.

"Good Fortune"

"Read, stranger. . . . When you have learned that he alone is free who is personally free, you will get precious provisions for your journey. Do you want to evaluate a man's freedom? Look at his very nature: //{5} is he free interiorly? do his judgments start from a right reason? That's what makes true nobility. Furnished with this criterion for discerning a man's freedom, consider stuff and nonsense the long list of ancestors that some boast of. No, ancestors do not found a man's freedom. //{10} For there is but one and the same ancestor for all, Zeus, and but one and the same origin, for all, and the same mud has been used for all. The man who has been allotted a noble nature is the true gentleman, the genuine free man. On the other hand, I am not afraid to call a slave, even thrice a slave -- even if he boasts about his ancestors - the mean man who possesses only a craven soul.

"// {15} Stranger, Epictetus was born of a slave mother. He was an eagle [12] among men, a spirit very renowned for his wisdom. What shall I call him? He was a godlike man. Would to heaven that today again in response to the world's prayers there might be born from a slave mother a man identical to him, a powerful help, a marvelous cause for joy for mortals."

NOTES

1. *B.* = Bailey, *U.* = Usener, *G.V.* = *Gnomologium Vaticanum,Ep.* = *Epistula* following the numbering of Diogenes Laertius. In these quotations "complete independence" translates, for want of a better word, the Greek *autarkeia.* [I have added in parentheses our more common English translation "self-sufficiency" -- Trans.]

2. I have retained with Bignone the text of the manuscript: *kompous* and not *kompou, sobarous,* and not *aphobous* (Usener) or *asobarous* (Leopold).

3. *Sunkatheis* Usener. If the *sunkritheis* of the manuscript is retained with Bignone, the sense is "When the wiseman is perfectly combined with . . ." so as to make a perfect mixture.

4. *S.V.F.* = *Stoicorum Veterum Fragmenta* of Von Arnim. I refer to volume and number.

5. Chrysippus, *en tôi prôtôi peri pronoias* (in the first book of his *On Providence*): "Only the world is said to be completely independent (self-sufficient, *autarkês*) because it alone possesses in itself everything it needs (cf. Plato, *Timaeus,* 33 d 2). It nourishes itself and increases of itself while all of its parts transform into one another," *S.V>F.,* II, 604.

6. Strained or flexed like a nerve or muscle: *eneurôse.*

7. This is the common teaching of the School; cf. too Antipater of Tarsus, Fr. 56, *S.V.F..,* III, 252, 30.

8. *nomimê epitropê, S.V.F.,* III, 544.

9. *Hermes* XXIII (1888), 542-543 (Kaibel). -- Naturally the passages on freedom in Seneca, Marcus Aurelius, and others should be added to this

list. For Seneca, see especially *Ep.*, 75, 18, *de prov.*, 1, 5; 6, 6.

10. It is noteworthy that these authors, especially Dio Chrysostom and Epictetus (see Von Arnim's index, p. 365, and that of Schenkl) make great use of the example of Socrates who was for them the very model of the wise man. The Stoic of the *Tusculan Disputations* already had said: "The Stoic philosophers have accurately preserved the Socratic tradition" (III, 5, 10). The statement in the *Apology* and the *Republic* (cf. *supra,* note 4 of Chapter I. C): "Nothing evil befalls the wiseman," is endlessly repeated by the Stoa in the form: "Nothing evil bothers the wise man," cf. *S.V.F.*, III, 567 ff., particularly 570 (=Cicero, *Tusc.* III, 10, 21): *abest ergo a sapiente aegritudo (pathos)*: "the wise man has no care." This is the famous Stoical *apatheia* and Socrates becomes its perfect model. Lucian's *Demonax* marvelously expresses this trend: when questioned about happiness, Demonax replies "Only the free man is happy, that is to say, the man who no longer has any hope for, or fear of anything whatsoever" (XXXVII, 20). And when he was asked which philosopher he preferred, he replied: "All deserve admiration, but personally I revere Socrates, admire Diogenes, and love Aristippus" (*ibid.*, 62). On Socrates' treatment of life as a game (already in Plato, *Symposium,* 216 d-e), cf. Epictetus, *Discourses,* II, 5, 18 (where Meletus should be read instead of Anytos), IV, 7, 30-31, and Plotinus, *Enneads,* III, 2, 15.

11. Oldfather, in his edition of Epictetus, *Loeb Classical Library,* I, (1926) xvii.

12. *aie[tos]* Sterret: *hage[môn]* Kaibel, "this guide of men."

II

COMMUNITY AND THE GREEK CITY

The notion of community is intimately connected with the notion of city as understood by the Greek philosophers and the Christian doctors of the Middle Ages. For, no matter how we consider it, the notion of community necessarily implies the idea of participation. This participation can be either of the material or spiritual order: we can join together for the joint management of the same property; but we can also unite so that as a group we may develop and bring to ultimate perfection all of our properly human faculties -- our intellectual faculties. The first type of society is concerned only with "living" *(to zên)*. Greece was familiar with such associations, but only in private life. The Greek sages did not consider it worthwhile to limit their thought to this level. The second type of society is concerned with "living well" *(to eu zên)*. It is the second type that gives rise to the notion of the city. From the very beginnings of philosophy, the Greek sages always considered this phenomenon with great care; for the attainment of man's end depends upon good constitutions and just government. That end consists in bringing to perfection what makes man a man, his reason or, to translate the word *nous* more accurately, the intellect which is in him and which puts him in harmony with the divine Intellect.

For purposes of *eu zên*, (living well) however, this partnership clearly implies that citizens share proportionately *(en harmonia)*, but by no means equally, that ideal which comprises the goal sought. The fifth-century Greek city is, in a true sense, a Church or, if you prefer, a sort of religious order. Like an order, it is exclusive. It is not precisely content with the mere physical presence of a certain number of individuals gathered into one and the same place, but rather demands much more: communion of souls and work in common (each in its proper sphere) in pursuit of the good which all are striving to realize and which can be attained only by unanimous endeavor.

Thus it follows that civic life necessarily demands the practice of the moral virtues. "Such is, in my opinion, the end which man must always have before his eyes in order to give direction to his life. Every man must direct all his energies, all those of the state, towards this end, the acquisition of justice and temperance as necessary for happiness, and he must relate all his action to this end" (Plato, *Gorgias*, 507 d-e). It all fits together: true happiness is the happiness of our spiritual being. This happiness can be realized only through civic society. Such society demands that each man aim at one and the same goal: the good of the whole: "No one is to let his desires be unrestrained and consent to a life of crime to satisfy his insatiable appetite. *Such a man can be loved by neither other men nor the gods. He is incapable of entering into community. Now, where there is no community, there can be no friendship" (Gorgias, 507 e).*

The conclusion, then, is that the notion of civic community leads to the notion of civilization. In Greece, the idea of *civilization* was born in and spread from the *city.* The principal elements of the concept of civilization, their arrangement, and, so to speak, their genealogy are treated in the short study which follows. First we shall try to discover what the complex notion of *eu zên* (living well), as realized in the city, meant to a fifth- or fourth-century Greek. Then we shall attempt to show that, far from rejecting the data of pure reason, the teaching of the Christian doctors confirms them, justifies them, and finally gives them a fuller meaning thanks to the contribution of the Gospel.

A. CIVILIZATION IN THE GREEK CITY

1º Civilization comes from *civilis*: "someone who belongs to the city, someone who can live as a sociable individual." The second meaning comes form the first; for an individual's usefulness enables him to *take his place in a group which constitutes a city. Both meanings are* common, both render the Latin *civilis* and the Greek *politikos,* which *civilis* translates (Polybius, 23, 5, 7; 18, 48, 7). Thus we are lead to the source: the Greek idea of *polis.* If we look at the beginnings and origin of "civilization," we will have a better chance of understanding it clearly (Aristotle, *Pol.* I, 2. 1252 a 24). [1]

2º The details and complex phenomena of the city's development are obscure, but the logical lines of the evolution are quite clear. In a word, it is the transition from arbitrary domination by the clan-chieftain to authorized rule of law which assures every member of one and the same group complete equality in duty and privilege.

Let us review the facts. From about the middle of the third millenium to 1000 B.C. warrior hordes repeatedly swept down upon the peninsula of Hellas. The invaders' social unit was the family, made up of all the descendants of the same ancestor and linked by one and the same cult around one and the same altar. It was the patriarchal clan *(patria* or *genos).* Naturally several families united. Their flocks grazed side by side on the same plains where they had pitched their tents, they travelled and fought together, these companions in arms were on good terms with one another and formed societies of "brothers" *(phratriai).* Finally, on large expeditions, this host of nomadic phratries (brotherhoods) divided into a small number of tribes.

These immigrants took possession of land and settled down, driving out the original inhabitants or reducing them to semi-slavery. Then in the ordinary course of human events this original inequality became more pronounced. With the passage of time members of an individual clan inevitably had different experiences. Some became rich; oth-

ers poorer. The latter sold their fields or, if they continued to work
them, paid rent. If they had a bad year, they had to borrow. When they
were insolvent, their creditor sold them along with their wives and children into slavery. These wretched people invoked justice in vain. For
the"kings" or clan-chieftains, who were necessarily rich and powerful,
sat in judgment. Hesiod mentions their "crooked judgments," and
speaks of the hawk devouring the nightingale. Be patient. There is justice: she is the dauther of Zeus and immortal. Wounded by men's
crimes, she is taking refuge in heaven by her Father's side. Zeus will
inflict punishment (Hesiod, *Erga*, 202 ff., 219 ff., 252 ff.).

    Soon, during the seventh-century the unfortunate peasants,
mariners, and small artisans banded together. But they would probably
have remained impotent had they not made an alliance with the port-
dwellers. The latter had become rich through commerce, but, because
they were younger sons, or illegitimate, or offspring of plebeians, were
not members of the nobility and were thus, without rights. Hereafter a
new force arose, the *dêmos* (the people). Dêmos and oligarchs engaged
in a lengthy conflict. A kind of innate wisdom, however, finally led the
Greeks to discover the principle which will simultaneously found the
city and beget civilization -- the idea of law.

    3° As the Greeks viewed it, law, as something human, was
relative or conditional in origin, but once established law assumed an
absolute value because of its imperative character. [2]

    Law is relative because it is the creation of men who have
united in a given place and time to solve the precise difficulties of that
time and place. From the beginning, law is seen as a compromise between adversaries. As Solon expressed it: law lays no claim to infalli-
ble perfection, but only to pure convenience. Because life is constantly
changing and the balance of powers is susceptible to change, law is capable of reform: law is a constant adjustment (Aristotle, *Pol.*, II, 8,
1268 b 31 ff.). All that has to be done is to begin anew what was done
before: the parties should meet again, take stock of their needs and
jointly seek a middle course. The Greek was so acutely aware of law's
relativity in the face of the "dynamism" of human affairs that he was
willing to take for granted such confrontations. On certain days
throughout the year, the Athenian Assembly had as its *agendum*, the re-
vision of laws. In peace treaties, certain Greek States stipulated that at
fixed times their ambassadors would meet again to rework the treaty in
accordance with new conditions.

Law's singular value and specific distinction in the Greek's eyes consisted in this: law is based on mutual consent. Until the birth of the city, the will of an individual or of a small group was imposed upon the masses. However, the privileged classes of monarchs or oligarchs did not aim at the good of the whole, at the common interest (Arist., *Eth. Nic.,* V, 6, 1134 b 1 ff.). Obedience could be secured only through violence and such a regime of violence necessarily gave rise to a state of rebellious feeling. Disorder was prevalent. On the other hand, because law had for its object the good of all -- this is proper to its definition -- everyone would accept it. They had submitted to force, but now they freely obeyed. And this free obedience in its turn gave birth to order. Freedom, consent, and order are precisely the constitutive elements of civic government. No longer are there masters and slaves. Now there are only free men who are striving to establish justice (*Eth., Nic.* V, 6, 1134 a 25 ff.).

As long as there was discussion, each party might refuse to give its pledge. But this pledge, once given, was binding. The law had to assume a stable character; for without it no order was possible. Here we have the source of the law's absolute value or, if you prefer, its *static* value. It does not take much reflection to realize that the law possesses this value of its very nature. By nature, a law is to be a rational and freely accepted agreement; for we can imagine only two types of society: either authority comes from one man who imposes his will on a passive multitude or this authority derives from common agreement. In the latter case, however, rights imply duties and the first duty is honesty. We cannot say *yes* and then act as if we had said *no*. No human society has a chance to survive when its members intend to go back on their word, once given. If Athens' laws displease Socrates, he has two options: he can go to the Assembly, criticize the laws, and propose better ones, or he can leave Athens. But if, conscious of his rights, he stays at Athens, he accepts her laws. He is therefore, bound by them. His mere presence in the city is equivalent to an oath. Socrates cannot perjure himself. Perjury is, of course, physically possible, but not morally so. Indeed, it is the specific character of the notion of law to demand a choice: will a man live in society in conformity with a moral order or does he prefer the regime of the wild beast which depends only on might to satisfy its hunger?

4º The foundation of law finally becomes clear. It is reason, that capacity which the Greeks liked to think had been given to every

man as the distinctive mark of what made him a man. Applied to the
"political animal," that is to say, to man living in society, reason is
called *justice* and the establishment of justice is the proper function of
man to the degree that he tries to fulfill his true nature. Thus the consequence of law is to consecrate this just order by inserting it into custo-
mary behavior. To have a body and to become an incarnate reality, the
idea has to strive for perfection in an institution. But at this point, let
us hear an ancient author:

> Man's life, whether he lives in a small or a large city, is
> governed by nature and by law. Whereas nature differs and
> varies with the individual, laws are something which are
> common, regulated, and identical for all....They aim at the
> just, the beautiful, and the useful: that is their goal. And
> when they have found it, they cast it in a statute which is
> universal, uniform, and equal for all. That is what law is.
> Everyone owes it obedience for it is the city's common con-
> tract to which all the city's members are obliged to conform
> their lives (Ps.- Demosthenes, *C. Aristog.* I, 15-16).

5º Justice or law goes hand in hand with order and this union between law and order comes from law's dependence upon reason
(Plato, *Laws,* IV, 713 e - 714 a: Aristotle, *Pol.* III. 16. 1287 a 32).
Order, however, expresses the individual's membership, position, and
duties in a community. Order, therefore, is inseparable from "number"
(in the Greek sense) and "the mean": not to exceed the mean is the
great precept of wisdom. Now, when analyzed, this idea of mean also
reveals two component notions. It implies *collaboration* with a particular group and supposes a concommitant concern for a common interest.
But this implies in return that each member of the whole, as useful to
the group, constitutes a *moral person.* This latter fact essentially con-
fers upon him the absolute right to exist.

The concept of order which underlies the idea of justice contains the following elements: community and proportional rights in
this community founded precisely on the notion of a moral person.

This is verified in the individual in the city -- and thus civil
law is established.

This is true of the city in the totality of cities -- and thus in-
ternational law is established.

Finally, this is verified in the world itself which establishes an order *(kosmos)* which is able to last only because of the balance of its parts.

This second point is worth delay. Let us investigate the source of the city's claim to be a moral person. This point is essential. There have been great and small cities. There are great and small nations. But the strong have always tended to devour the weak. In the fifth-century, Athens devoured the Melians. Yet the Melians protested and this protest, as related by Thucydides (V, 85-113), may rightly be called the charter of civilization. For the historian himself remarked (with regard to the troubles in Corcyra, III, 82-83) that from the day when certain principles were no longer obeyed, civilization ceased to exist.

> a) To exist as a moral person, the city must first of all exist as a physical person: it must have a place and the possibility of not only coming into being, but of attaining well-being in this place.

> b) The second condition is a lawful adherence to certain patterns of life, of thought, of feeling, to a certain language, to customs and to its own cults, in short, to everything which we call, in a derived sense, a "national civilization."

> c. This very adherence, as long as it lasts and retains its will to fight, constitutes its best title to the right to exist. And this right becomes completely clear when this will to self-defence is, if necessary, put to the test of blood.

Thus the city is defined as a *moral person* established in a certain place which affords it sufficient resources for life and a good life; the proof of duration testifies to its capacity for life and legitimizes its right; even though overwhelmed by superior force, its right remains. This city has become part of an order, has collaborated with a whole. To suppress it, by an act of violence and in pursuance of sheerly violent motives, constitutes an injustice, a *disorder*.

6º It is worthwhile to note one of the principal consequences of these doctrines: the appearance of the *natural law* or of "natural justice" *(physikon dikaion)* which, according to Aristotle (*Eth. Nic.*, V, 7, 1134 b 18), has the same force everywhere and, whether accepted or not, remains always valid.

Law and Nature are at first presented as antagonistic terms, and a work of Antiphon as well as some famous passages from the *Republic* have placed this opposition in relief. This is, of course, what the Sophists were teaching in Athens in the second half of the fifth-century. Nature bids the strong to crush the weak, it urges the following of instinct, it exalts the will-to-power. Every act according to nature is, therefore, a good act. And the endorsement of the natural act's goodness is the success of the stronger. On the other hand, Law represents the coalition of the weak. Just as two forces balance each other, the multitude, by their number, counterbalances the will of the tyrant. Suppose the multitude triumphs, the result is just despotism backwards. And since there is no middle term between such divergent forces, the history of the people actually is, and of necessity can be nothing other than a series of sudden changes: unending struggle, the expression of life itself. These theories which seduced the Athenian nobles had their practical effects. Athens experienced them when she emerged in ruin from the Peloponnesian War. Then it was that Plato, in order to save his country, began to seek a metaphysical principle which would serve as an unshakable foundation for justice.

This is not the place to recall this inquiry. Let us show only what its consequences were for natural law. If there exists a true Being, the immutable, eternal Idea of the Good, of the Beautiful, and of the Just, if Man is in communication with the Idea only in so far as he possesses an intellective soul of the same nature as the Idea, it follows that, for man, living according to his true nature is the same thing as conforming himself to Being, modeling himself on the Just. Consequently, when we speak of "natural law," it is no longer necessary to think of this blind and mechanical Nature which regulates the universe's phenomena and instinct's impulses. It is a question of man's nature *qua* its essential note, of man in as much as he is spirit. However, since this nature is common to all men, there is also a law, certain moral principles, which every man ought to acknowledge solely because he is a man. Hence, we come to the idea of a universal society of humans, ruled by unwritten but imprescriptible laws: such is the meaning of the natural law.

This principle has, however, some very weighty consequences. If we admit that all men are equally conscious of a certain number of moral rules, every act against these rules is destined to have repercussions on the universal conscience. By itself, this conscience already passes judgment on the horror aroused by crime: it has the weight of sanction. But there is a more direct sanction: this occurs when a people takes up arms in defense of another people, not because they have themselves experienced some injustice, but because they can not bear to have an injustice committed. In this case, war is not only legitimate: it is a highly moral act: it expresses the most pure ideal of the human conscience. [3]

7º These Greek ideas experienced an amazing stroke of fortune from the day on which Alexander ordered his Hellenic soldiers to marry the daughters of the Persians. The facts are clear: city and civilization have progressed at the same pace. As Alexander and then the Diadochi, and then the Empire, founded new cities in lands, till then without culture, the Barbarians of Pontus, of Africa, or of Germany learned to govern themselves more wisely, to practice justice, to be human. In 212, Caracalla extended the benefits of the *civitas* to all the free inhabitants of the Empire. The small Greek city became the city of the world. Under the aegis of *libertas,* and thanks to the **Pax Romana**, men aspired to form a world society: *Urbem fecisti quod prius orbis erat* (What was previously the world, you have made a city).

If the limits of this article do not permit a treatment of this noble subject, [4] we must at least state what Christianity's attitude ought to be with regard to civilization -- I mean this just order, sanctioned by law, in a spirit of community which ultimately is founded upon a common human nature.

NOTES

1. The French used to express this same idea with the word *police.* Its Greek source *(politeia)* is obvious. [cf. English "policy = prudent conduct;" Trans.]

2. The next section sticks quite closely to the writings of Plato and Aristotle. A reference should be made on every line, but the reader who is familiar with Greek thought will easily recognize the sources.

3. Such a feeling was already found in outline in the fourth-century in the Amphictyonic League and the assistance which all Greeks gave the citizens of Delphi against their Phocian invaders.

4. A summary of come characteristics may be found in "Community and *Romanitas*" infra.

B. CIVILIZATION AND CHRISTIANITY

"Finally, brethren, whatever is true, whatever is honorable, whatever is just, whatever is pure, whatever is lovely, whatever is gracious, if there is any excellence, if there is anything worthy of praise, think about these things" (*Phil.* 4.8) This is the golden rule of Christianity. Far from seeking to destroy what reason had prescribed, it took it up, and conferred upon it a divine value.

St. Paul is proud of belonging to the city of Tarsus (*Acts* 21.39). He argues about his title to Roman citizenship (*Acts* 16.37; 22.25, 29). Of course, he declares that "Our Commonwealth is in heaven" (*Phil.* 3.20), to recall the final end: he certainly does not wish to overthrow the terrestrial order. He profits from this order, he uses his civic rights, and he recognizes the duties which are imposed by and are legitimate counterparts of these rights. "Therefore, one must be subject (to those in authority), not only to avoid God's wrath but also for the sake of conscience" (*Rom.* 13.5 and the entire chapter). Within its due limits, and on condition that it does not overstep these limits, authority comes from God. A conflict can arise only if authority goes beyond, or encroaches upon the rights of God.

This constant doctrine leaves the Christian completely free to define the norms of civilization. On this problem there has never been any disagreement between the Roman Church and the separated churches. Since they recognize one and the same natural law, "written on their hearts" (*Rom.* 2.14-16), they necessarily agree. The important voices raised during the Hitler war, Protestant or Catholic, spoke the same language. Thus, if we now appeal to the writings of a medieval Catholic theologian, we do so for the sake of convenience and not as a rejection of other excellent works.

Social life is a *natural* endowment: man reaches his own perfection and happiness only by living in society (St. Thomas, *Summa Theol.*, I. q. 96, a. 4).

The foundation of this life is *reason*. What constitutes the social body is not an imperative will -- even if this were divine -- or *a fortiori* that of some prince, but the same concern, in all parts of the whole, for the common good. Consequently, the structure is not artificial: it is held together by an organic bond. The will of an individual creates a tyranny, not an order; the common will of everyone, the expression of an identity of nature, creates law: *ordinatio rationis in bonum commune* (an ordinance of reason for the common good) (I-II, q. 90, a. 1).

Hence it follows that the social order is, of its essence, *moral*. Its constraint is not external; it obliges in the forum of conscience, since it touches man's spirit in its very desire for perfection (I-II, q. 96, a. 4). Freedom, therefore, is its first prerequisite. True order demands consent of the parties, consent demands free concurrence, and man is never better entitled to use his right than when he tries to increase the desire for perfection inherent in his nature (I-II, q. 96, a. 5).

Here we have revealed the ultimate *spiritual* dimension of law and of order, and of the interior discipline which a free being feels honored to accept (I-II, q. 96, a. 6).

Such is the nature of the civil order, great or small, whether it is limited to one State or encompasses a group of States. It is an objective order: it rests upon a reality -- *identical human nature*. For this is quite definitely the crux of the problem. Either we recognize this identity of nature and acknowledge at the same time that all have an equal right to live and equal obligations or we deny it, and the only thing left is the will-to-power. When a man or a State sees itself and itself alone as superior by nature and privileged in some regard it can no longer limit its will. Those who oppose its designs no longer have the right to be called men. Its decree constitutes the Good, the True, and the Just. All the traditional values take on a new meaning. At this point, a choice must be made. The idea of *civilization* and the concept of the *superman* have nothing in common.

Let us keep the faith of old Hesiod, this patrimony which has come from the dawn of time and which the Church preserves. The spirit has a law which can never perish. Perhaps in this world, from time to time, injustice may seem to rule. But merely let the just be sacrificed for their cause: they will not die in vain. The flame of civilization may no longer be visible, it may be believed dead; but it smoulders beneath the ashes and one day it will spring to life and blaze up more beautifully than every before.

III

COMMUNITY AND *ROMANITAS*

In the course of a few centuries, human history saw the development of a community which went beyond the framework of the small autonomous city to stretch to the ends of what was then called the *oikoumenê,* that is to say not only "the inhabited world" (as it is usually translated), but the world governed by laws which were consonant with reason, in a word, "the civilized world." This was the Roman community, the *Romanitas.* This was a community in the proper sense, since all of its members really participated in public affairs and were aware of this participation. As a matter of fact, they were the entire urban population, all the citizens of the towns in the Empire which had the rank of *civitates* and were administered by means of elected magistrates.

The progress which led to this reality and the awareness of this reality ended with the first century of our era. Emperors, magistrates or simple citizens, the authors of this time and of the second century, Pliny the Elder, Tacitus, Dio Chrysostom, Pliny the Younger, Aelius Aristides, Marcus Aurelius, have a very lively sense of working together at one and the same work, of "serving" one and the same cause, the cause of the good of the whole. This participation is eminently a "cult": Pliny the Elder had already said, *"Deus est mortali iuvare mortalem"* (It is divine for a mortal to help a mortal). There is no question of constraint imposed by the Supreme Authority on an amorphous mass of subjects, but of collaboration, of the gift of the entire person to the collective work.

This was, after all, the resurrection of the old concept of the city as understood by Plato and Aristotle, but infinitely more rich and more human, since the city now included men of all lands, of every race, whose bond was no longer birth and blood, but *a common education.* This is the essential fact. Because they were formed from infancy according to one and the same spiritual program the members of the *Romanitas* felt jointly responsible. But the more this community rested upon the spirit rather than the material the better chance it had of survival. The Roman Empire collapsed but the idea of *Romanitas* survived throughout all of the Middle Ages; it became "Christianity." Even today, "Graeco-Roman Civilization," "The West," and "Latinity" are not meaningless words

We have here attempted to analyze the components of *Romanitas,* not so much its "political" aspect, but rather the spiritual influence which it exerted on Europe and which remains its true value.

A. LATINITY IS NOT THE SAME AS IMPERIALISM

Latinity has sometimes been equated with imperialism: *Tu regere imperio populos, Romane, memento,* (You Roman, remember to rule the nations with authority.) The true heirs of Rome, the true Latins, are then seen as those who would wish to force themselves on Europe or even the entire universe in the name of superiority.

This thesis is easily refuted. First, the progress of Roman conquests is a very complex phenomenon and there is no certitude that it was due principally to a plan of domination, to a will-to-power on the part of the Roman Senate (cf. the generally accepted thesis of Mr. Holleaux). Second, it is always dangerous to make unqualified transfers from the realities of the past to existing facts. Just as the concept of the Greek city cannot be simply applied as it is to our modern democracies, so a modern conqueror cannot extend his dominion over an ever greater area in order to continued the Roman Empire.

Rome faced either barbaric tribes or composite monarchies which had no bond of internal cohesion. On the contrary, every modern state which tends toward imperialism faces other states no less lawfully constituted which have equal claims to be moral persons.

Moreover, even on the political plane there is a second quite appreciable difference between the Roman Empire and modern imperialism. No matter how it may have been established, the Roman Empire continued to exist in so many provinces and for so many centuries, only because it was a guarantee of peace: *Pax Romana!* And this Roman peace lasted only because of the *liberality* of the Roman government. Rome had the genius to understand that the large body over which she presided would be an *order* only if all the parts of this body adhered to the whole spontaneously and were freely established in one and the same whole. Hence, she gave the provinces the true liberties: liberty of speech, of religion, of finances, of justice, of government. And in places where these liberties were non-existent, for example, among the small tribes who had lived till then under tribal regime, Rome created them by setting up *municipia* (free towns). Rome taught the barbarians to govern themselves. Far, then, from imposing herself by force, Rome prevailed by justice. And hence she endured. The weak garrisons which she maintained in the provinces would have been annihilated in a single day if the Roman subjects had really decided to revolt. Quite to the contrary, they had only one desire -- to become more Roman. And Rome complied with this desire. In 212, Caracalla made all the free men of the Empire Roman citizens. In the fourth century, a very expressive word, *Romania,* indicates the results of this policy: "the fusion between the widely different people subjugated by Rome has become complete: they are all recognized as members of one single nation" (G. Paris). Henceforth, to be "Roman" means to be conformed to a certain manner of thinking, of feeling, and of living which expresses a human ideal: and this idea is so lively, and has taken such firm root, that, even after the sack of Rome by Alaric, in 410, a poet could still write: "What was previously the world, you have made a city," *Urbem fecisti quod prius orbis erat.*

B. LATINITY REPRESENTS A "HUMAN" IDEAL

What then is the human ideal symbolized by "Latinity"? Once more, it is not a political doctrine. We are and we remain different, citizens of different lands. The "Latin" community is of a spiritual order. In the fifth century, a Latin from Spain, the historian Paul Orosius, seems to me to have defined its significance exactly: "Wherever I go, should I know no one, I am at peace, I do not fear violence. *I am a Roman among Romans, a Christian among Christians, a man among men.* Community of laws, of beliefs, of nature, protects me: in every land I recognize the fatherland."

This quotation completely sums up our debt to Rome. Rome did not pride herself on privilege of race. As early as the end of the first century, she permitted government by emperors of mixed blood, or even complete strangers: Trajan and Hadrian were Spaniards, Antoninus was of Gallic origin, Septimius Severus came from Africa, Diocletian from Dalmatia. Moreover, Rome never dreamt of "Latinizing" the conquered provinces by deporting the natives and replacing them with Latins. It is an almost unbelievable, but nevertheless true fact that authors as purely "Roman" as Saint Cyprian, Tertullian, St. Augustine, were Berbers; probably not one drop of Latin blood coursed through their veins.

Rome never claimed cultural superiority: the conquered Greeks became her teachers; she went to their school. The significance of this fact is incalculable. I would venture to say that it is precisely this fact that is the origin of the bond of "Latinity." As a matter of fact, it is to her very humility that Rome owes the fact that she in turn became a great civilizing force, whose influence is still felt. She did not imagine that she, and she alone, possessed all truth. She admitted that other people before her, had made contributions to the formation of this precious human treasure, the great ideas of law, order, and peace, which are the basis of our civilization. Instead of denying them, or destroying them, Rome strove to serve them. Cicero translated Plato. He was inspired by him on every page. All of his reflections on political life, virtue and happiness flow from principles conceived by men of another race. He spread them in magnificent language. And look at his reward. This beautiful Latin prose becomes the vehicle of wisdom. Cicero became the student of the Greeks to instruct Rome: he did not instruct only Rome -- I mean his contemporaries -- but all the Latin authors who were to follow. The pagans and the Christians, and then, directly or indirectly the Fathers, the entire middle ages and the Renaissance. Since his works were going to become the "Classics" *par excellence* in the school system created in the sixteenth century, and subsequently stabilized by the Jesuits, and handed on to us by the lycea of Napoleon, the Latins have brought us all human wisdom, both social and individual.

Such is a first meaning of the word "Latinity" and even now we understand how in this sense it expresses the ideal of man. No longer is any isolated being, any race, any country in sole possession of the body of human truths. Civilization is a common work in which all collaborate. It is a work which is slowly accomplished through labor and trials, and in which all new progress supposes learning as a beginning: it is at the basis of education. Greece educated Rome; then Rome, the West. Hence it follows that "Latinity" is the equivalent of "humanity": to put oneself outside of this Latin society is, in some way, to exclude oneself from the human community.

C. LATINITY REPRESENTS A "CHRISTIAN" IDEAL

It is no accident that the enemies of Latin humanism are also the enemies of Christianity. This enmity is enlightening. The two ideas are actually connected. Indeed the Christians themselves were not slow to see this and to make themselves champions of Roman civilization.

The reason for this is not just on the material, political, or linguistic order. Doubtless, as the Christian apologists as early as the end of the fourth century, took pleasure in showing, [1] Roman political unity was very useful for the spread of the Gospel: *didicerunt omnes homines, sub uno terrarum imperio viventes, unius Dei omnipotentis imperium fideli eloquio confiteri,* (all men living under one worldly authority learned to recognize in a firm declaration the authority of one omnipotent God). (St. Ambrose, *Enarrat. in Ps.,* XLV, 21). Moreover, the head of Christianity, Peter's heir and vicar of the Son of God, was established at Rome, the seat of the Empire. And finally, Latin, the administrative language of the imperial governments was from the third century (till then Greek was in use) the official language of the liturgy.

But these are not the principal reasons. The Church sent her missionaries into distant lands where the name of Rome had never been heard. The successor of Peter could stay at Avignon and still remain the head of the Church. Greeks, Syriacs, Coptics, Armenians, Slavonics have been able to translate the public prayer of the Roman Church without losing the fundamental unity of the Christian community. The essential element lies elsewhere. The Empire had already accustomed the people of the "inhabited world" to consider themselves as one people: they would compose an order under the great rule of *aequitas* (equity); they would enjoy a freedom which would make them promote this order -- *concordia* (harmony); and they would feel united by this mutual good-will, this natural love of man for his fellow creatures, which the fine word *humanitas* (humanity) expresses. The ground, then, was all ready for the announcement of a religion which declared all men children of the same Father, brothers of Jesus Christ, the Son of God.

Let us not hesitate to assert that these ideas of unity, of catholicity have civilized the world. The invincible conviction that there exists a natural relationship in all rational beings has led the Church to educate the barbarians when they invaded the Empire and destroyed the Roman order, and when to all appearances civilization was dead. Confidently believing that the barbarian was perfectible, since he was a man, the Church undertook this great task, the most noble in this world, of forming the completely inexperienced minds, the savage but upright hearts of the infidel invaders. And thus, thanks to popes, bishops, and monks, "Latinity" survived. Once again it set up a human community in which each man, each Christian could recognize a brother in his neighbor of another race. Even today, if we aspire to a human society it is on the lines of these principles which have guided in turn the Greek sages, the Roman magistrates, and the doctors and apostles of Christianity.

NOTE

1. Prudentius, Orosius, Cyril of Alexandria, St. Jerome, St. John Chrysostom, Prosper of Aquitaine, St. Leo: cf. Labriolle in Fliche-Martin, *Histoire de l'Eglise*, IV, 360, n. 1.

IV

AUTARKY AND COMMUNITY

IN ANCIENT GREECE

1) "Autarky" (which must not be confused with "autarchy") comes from the Greek *autarkeia* which signifies the quality or state of being self-sufficient (*autarkeia*) and of constituting by oneself an independent unity. Therefore autarky is equivalent to self-sufficiency, especially in the economic order, but also on other levels.

The word has a twofold history. In moral reflection it is linked to the problem of beatitude which greatly preoccupied Greek thought. As a matter of fact, whatever beatitude's essence may be, it is quite clear that one of its primary conditions is the absence of all privation. Privation involves suffering. Man, therefore, ought to be self-sufficient, he ought to be independent, in the image of God, [1] "the perfectly happy one." Autarky is, as it happens, one of beatitude's distinctive characteristics.

Autarky is thus an integral part of beatitude and the end of human life could just as well be called either happiness or self-sufficiency. (Cf. Hecataeus of Abderus, DK 73 A 4 -- Plato, *Phil.*, 67 a [neither the soul nor pleasure constitutes happiness in themselves since they cannot be self-sufficient]; *Republic*, III, 387 d-e [the wise man is self-sufficient for the good life; he is more than all the others independent, cf. *Menex.*, 247 e]; Plato is fond of expressing this same idea of sufficiency by the words *hikanos, hikanotês*, cf. *Lys.*, 215 a; *Phil.*, 19 e, 22 b, 52 d, 60 d-e, 66 b, 67 a -- Aristotle *Rhet.*, I, 5. 1360 b 15 [one

[one of the definitions of happiness is independence of life], *Eth. Nic.*, I, 7. 1097 b 7 ff. [The perfect good includes autarky: cf. *Rhet.*, I, 6, 1362 a 27].)

Now, since the idea of privation is immediately connected with that of desire, and since desire is insatiable, it follows that the happy man knows how to moderate his desires, to limit them just to goods indispensable for existence. "Life abroad teaches autarky (self-sufficiency, *Genügsamkeit*): gruel, a bed of straw are welcome remedies for hunger and fatigue" (Democritus, 246 DK). "Chance affords a well-furnished table; moderation always bestows enough food" (*autarkea*, Democr., 210 DK). "Chance is lavish but inconstant; nature is self-sufficient *(autarkês)*, but with its mediocre but certain gifts it is more valuable than the beautiful promises of hope" (Democr., 176 DK). Epicurus gives the same advice (*Epist.*, III, 130-131; *Sent. Vat.*, 45, etc.; cf. also Arist., *Pol.*, I, 8, 1256 b 32). The Stoics would achieve the same goal by different means: by affirming that virtue is sufficient to make man happy (Zeno: *S.V.F.*, I, 46, 33; Antipater, *ib.*, III 252, 33, etc.). The wise man has no needs *S.V.F.*, III, 151, 30, 153, 17) because he possesses the perfect good, virtue (*Ib.*, III, 152, 35, 154, 15). In a word, on the moral plane, autarky is the privilege of God or of the world -- and, in his image, of the virtuous and perfectly happy man (Plato, Aristotle), of the Epicurean or Stoic wise man.

2) A sentence from Herodotus' famous dialog between Croesus and Solon (I, 32, 9) shows how the idea of autarky appeared on the economic and political levels and how it paralleled moral reflection: "Because of his human condition, man cannot have all goods at once; for just as no land can furnish itself with an adequate supply of goods -- a land has some things and lacks others and the land which has the most goods is the best -- so also no man is absolutely self-sufficient; but the man who has possessed most goods till the end of his life and has been able to bring his destiny to fulfillment, that man, O King, to my mind justly merits the name happy." This statement is worth remembering. No single individual (man or country) has the privilege of autarky. The good life demands joint forces. And, as a matter of fact, such is the essential origin of the city: "The origin of the city, in my opinion, ought to be sought in this fact that none of us is self-sufficient, but each lacks many things. . . . Hence, a man seeks another to satisfy one need, and yet another for another need, and being in need of many things, we have got together in one and the same dwelling

place to live together and to help one another, and to this common residence we have given the name of city. . . . Between one man and another there exists an exchange, each gives and receives, convinced that this exchange is most valuable for him. . . . What gives rise to the city, therefore, is our own needs" (Plato, *Rep.*, II, 369 b-c: cf. *Laws*, III, 676 a 1 ff.). This text does not force us to think that the city is limited to the satisfaction of life's necessities. For Plato, no less than for Aristotle, the end of the State and the individual is "well-living" (*Laws*, VIII, 828 d - 829 a). Aristotle's reproof (*Pol.* IV, 4, 1291 a 10 ff.) with regard to Plato (*Rep.*, II, 369 b ff.) is therefore unjustified. The Platonic State also has as its end the noble life *(to kalon)* but Plato, as is logical and natural, began with its foundation, that is to say the absolutely basic needs of existence.

Man's basic needs are nourishment, lodging, clothing, implying three classes: farmers, builders, weavers, (and shoe makers). And there is also a fourth, artisans who supply the first three with instruments indispensable for their work. We could add the cowherders, shepherds and other herders to tend beasts of burden (*Rep.*, II, 369 d - 370 e). Is that all? Is it possible to found a city in a location so full of resources that there would be no need to import anything? No. *Therefore, inter-city commerce must be instituted.* (370 e 10 ff.: cf. Herodotus, I, 32, 9, cited *supra*) and from this will follow a sixth class, merchants (mariners will be included here) and the necessity that "the State produce not only enough for its own needs, but also the kind of objects and in such number as to meet the demands of countries from which it imports the commodities it lacks" (370 e - 371 a). Such are the *natural* conditions of every civilized State. Aristotle makes clear the philosophical principles which justify these facts. Man is a social animal. Hence, if he tends toward beatitude, which implies self-sufficiency, this sufficiency includes in its turn community. "It is agreed that the perfect good is something which is self-sufficient. Now the idea of self-sufficiency does not apply to an isolated individual leading a solitary life; it includes parents, children, wife, and, in brief, friends and fellow citizens, since man is, by his nature, made to live in a city" (*Eth. Nic.*, I, 7, 1097 b 7 ff.). With an eye to defending the plurality of classes in the State (since State is not only a collection, but a whole), the Stagirite observes: "With regard to self-sufficiency, a family is better than an individual, a city better than a family, and, *theoretically, a city tends to be fully realized only from the moment when the community comprised of numerous members is self-sufficient*" (*Pol.*, II, 2, 1261 b 11 ff.).

This maxim is of considerable import: the more the community expands (we are not talking about a crowd), the more members there are to collaborate toward the same end, and the more well-being there is. The fitting final step, then, is this: to pass from the collaboration of families and classes in one and the same State to the collaboration of States in one and the same Society of States. It would be pleasant to indicate how the human conscience, even among the pagans, was directed toward the realization of this progress. For, on the one hand, since the fourth-century the Greek cities strove to unite in federations: and, on the other, after his conquests, Alexander's main plan, which was followed by many of his successors (in particular the Seleucids), was to blend Greeks and Barbarians in one and the same community which would ultimately embody all that belongs to common human nature.

3) Theoretically, the city surpassed the clan from a moral point of view. As a matter of fact the members of the city were united by a moral bond: the idea of one and the same common good in which all participated and which they, therefore, felt obliged to serve. At the beginning of the fifth-century, when Darius, and then Xerxes, invaded Hellas at the head of huge armies, the small Greek city, but newly formed, was called upon to prove its worth. It passed the test. Devoted to their freedom, ready to defend it at all costs, the Greeks drove back to Asia these hordes who differed in origin, language and religion, and were united only by the will of one master and not by a common ideal.

The struggle assumed a symbolic character; the government of the people by the people emerged from it strengthened. Since Athens incontestably presented the most authentic example of this form of government, since she had directed the defense operations, it was inevitable that her pride should become overweening. In her strength, she would no longer be content with affirming her rights: she would deny the rights of others. Doubtless, she would attempt to preserve this uneasy union of Greek States which the presence of the enemy had for a time effected; but she would establish it through violence and to her own profit. The first Athenian Confederacy was in no way a federation of free cities freely united with a view to the common good: it was an empire committed to Athenian interests alone.

For it would have been a federation in the true sense only if it had simultaneously safeguarded these two principles: the individual autonomy of each State and the subordination of the States to a larger organism whose authority would be decisive in legal disputes. Such a problem involved two juridical solutions. Both of them -- one extreme, the other less absolute -- were attempted in the Hellenistic period. The very names which were given to them indicate their characteristics: *isopolity* and *sympolity*. In the first case, common interests are so clear that the States making up the union reciprocally exchange civic rights: the inhabitants of Athens and Samos are equally citizens in both of these towns with the same rights and the same duties. In the second case, each city, while protecting its private interests, resolutely enters into a greater whole whose good appears to be superior to it in this sense, that it attains its own good only by contributing to the good of the whole. The Athenian citizen is a citizen in the proper sense only of Athens, but is given civic rights in the federal community.

The first solution seems fanciful and was never realized, except on a very small scale. the second was to prove the actual and legal formula for the future. As a matter of fact, it was the system of the double *civitas* (citizenship) which was able to assure so long a peace to the Roman Empire, because it was so firmly rooted in the free adherence of minds. But, it is quite obvious that to achieve this development, the city had to achieve wisdom. Athens was not able to see herself as only a part of a whole that was larger and better than herself when she conquered the barbarians and won this victory for her constitution. She wished to rule. She failed in this and lost her Empire. One of her noblest claims to glory is her understanding of her new position and of the state's true interests.

4) Indeed the Second Athenian Confederacy's specific difference can be summed up succinctly. In the first Confederacy the real power had passed from the Council of Allies (at first at Delos) to the Assembly of the Athenians. As a result, the same assembly wound up directing at the same time both Athenian affairs and those of the Confederacy. As a logical consequence, the Athenian Assembly, since it was completely occupied with the interests of the city, was inclined to use the Confederacy only to serve its own designs. Athens was no longer a part of the whole: there was no longer any whole. A confederacy presumes a common good. There was no longer any common good, only the good of Athens. It was truly an Empire which survived only through force. Athens imposed her own political regime on the Allies and, under the pretext of saving them from themselves or from the Persians or from the Spartans, sent them garrisons which divided among themselves the land of dispossessed citizens.

In the second Confederacy, each State kept its own assembly which was concerned with the private interests of the State. But each city at the same time sent delegates to a confederate *synedrion* (council) which was concerned with the interests of the whole. The delicate question was determining the relationship between these individual assemblies and the common *synedrion*. The former symbolize the cities' autonomy, the latter their desire for union. How, then, can we balance the claims of autonomy with the demands of the common good?

Greece never solved this problem and this failure caused its downfall. But the philosopher ought to learn from history. There is only one possible solution, namely the restraint of autonomy, especially on the issue of autocratically and unrestrainedly opting for peace or war. The idea of confederation necessarily involves that of arbitration. [2] The *synedrion's* right to arbitrate in its turn runs the risk of being only an empty dream, if it is not accompanied by true power founded, in practice, on a material force. Actually what happens if one of the disputing States refuses to accept the decision of the arbiters? Enforcement will be required. [3] The right of arbitration implies, therefore, a right of coercion, and so a common army and common finances. These needs create new problems concerning the just assessment of men and tribute, the leadership of the army, and so on. It is quite clear that the common good cannot be realized and maintained without sacrifices. But the example of Greece lies before us: because Greek cities did not learn to unite, they collapsed; because they never wished to sacrifice the smallest particle of their freedom they finally lost it all. This is an important lesson.

5) If from the fourth-century the Greek cities manifested a sincere desire for union, and if they made some laudable efforts to attain it, this union was limited to Greeks alone. The idea of Community still excluded the barbarians. "When Greeks fight with Greeks, this should not be called war, but sickness and discord: for all the Greek people are united by kinship, they have a common origin. Therefore, even in strife, they ought to spare one another, and not count as enemies all the inhabitants of a conquered city, men, women and children, but only the instigators of the dispute, who are always in the minority. They should wage hostilities as people destined for reconciliation. Looking upon the other Greeks, who are today their rivals, as brothers, they will correct them benevolently, without carrying chastisement as far as enslavement or destruction. For they will consider them friends who are to be reformed, not enemies. On the contrary, when Greeks fight with barbari-

ans, then there is real war, because they differ in race and blood and this
fact makes them natural enemies. Therefore in this war the Greeks will
employ against the barbarians the same cruel methods which they now
use against each other." So speaks Plato in the passage which I have
summarized (*Rep.*, V. 469 b - 471 c). His disciple Aristotle is of the
same opinion. In his *Politics* he shows that the despotic government,
which means reigning like a master over slaves, cannot be suitable for
the Greeks: for such a government would suppose so radical a difference in nature that the master would appear in a way to be a god in the
midst of men (III. 13. 1284 a 3-10). Such a difference, however, does
not exist among Greeks (V. 10. 1313 a 6 ff.), but only between Greeks
and barbarians, "for as far as their customs are concerned, the barbarians
are of a more servile nature than the Greeks, and the Asians than the
Europeans; and consequently it follows that they willingly support a despotic government and are not the least bit annoyed by it" (III. 14. 1285
a 20). The state of slavery, therefore, is at once, natural and good for the
barbarian (I. 5. 1254 b 16), just as it is natural and good for the body to
be the slave of reason: for the barbarian does not have reason which
alone renders the human being capable of freedom (1254 b 21 ff.). This
is the constant teaching. Certainly Isocrates praises Heracles for having
been the benefactor of all mankind (*Paneg.*, 56): but "all mankind" was
then equivalent to "all the Greeks" (*Philip.*, 114: cf. W. W. Tarn, *Alexander and the Unity of Mankind*, 30, n. 13). The same author advo-
cates unity (*homonoia*), but only among the Greeks, and recommends
their coalition against the barbarians under the command of the new
Heracles, Philip of Macedon as the best means to this union (*Paneg.*, 3,
cf. 184; *Panath.*, 163; *Phil.*, 114, 110).

On the contrary, let us take the words *hellênikos* (Greek),
hellênizein (to imitate the Greeks), *hellênismos* (imitation of the
Greeks), *hellênistês* (an imitator of the Greeks) in the sense in which
they are so frequently used in the Graeco-Roman era. They no longer
designate a race, but a way of life, open to all, Greek and barbarian. All
men are as a rule capable of this way of life, even if they do not all attain it at the same speed and to the same degree, even if they require
more or less education to reach it. At this time then, the distinguishing
characteristic for men is no longer race or blood but the fact that they
participate or do not participate in a certain "civility" or urbanity which
is acquired by education. Men are no longer Greeks or barbarians; they
are either civilized or uncivilized. A remark of Erastosthenes reveals this
new attitude at its best: "when certain men [4] were advising Alexander

to treat the Greeks as friends, and the barbarians as enemies, he was more correct in preferring to divide men into the good and the bad . . . , that is to say according to whether or not they allowed themselves to be guided by the prescriptions of law and by the principles of education and philosophical teaching." [5] This great revolution was the work of Alexander. The ancient authors assert it and a modern historian, W. W. Tarn, has demonstrated, in my opinion, that their assertion is well founded. Arrian declares (VII, 2 9) that when the Macedonians had been reconciled with Alexander after the rebellion at Opis, Alexander held a common banquet for the Macedonians and Persians, during which he prayed that the two people might live in concord and that they might share equally in the government. Plutarch shows that Alexander came as envoy of God to harmonize and reconcile all people. By blending ways of life and customs as if in one and the same bowl, he taught them to have but one fatherland, the earth, and to believe all good men their brothers, and only the wicked, strangers (*de Fortuna Alexandri*, I, 6). [6] Later (I, 8-9), Plutarch recalls Alexander's plan: to unite all men into one people by bringing all of them to union of hearts, to peace, and to good friendly understanding. Finally, elsewhere he cites the following expression of the prince: "God is the common father of all men" (*Vita Alexandri*, 27).

These were not empty words. In the cities founded by Alexander and his successors, especially in Asia, Greeks and Persians or Semites were equally citizens, enjoyed the same rights and held the same offices. In principle, a Hellenistic city gathered together in corporate bodies (*politeumata*) a group of Macedonians, some mercenaries and Greek merchants, some native born, sometimes some Thracians also, frequently some Jews. But it was not enough to gather them together: true fusion had to be achieved through marriage of the Greeks with the daughters of the natives. Alexander set an example by marrying Roxane. The name list of a Macedonian *katoikia* (colony) such as Doura shows how much this mixture of blood in the family -- the parent-cell of the city -- served to foster a sense of human community. [7] Everyone was educated at the gymnasium: there it was that civilized man was formed, that he learned to govern himself and to make himself worthy of "freedom." Public offices no longer demanded membership in one race, the Greek race; but it was necessary to have sat on the same benches as the sons of the Hellenes, to have taken part in their games, to have been trained as they were in the colleges of ephebes and of *neoi* (young men's clubs): in brief, it was necessary "to have hellenized." The Egyptian peasant is also seen leading his son to town that the child may profit from Greek education. From his own small town he sends him warm clothing, preserves, and the best wishes of his mother, but he takes great care also to exhort him not to waste his time. He himself is only a poor villager, but his boy will be "civilized"; he will be able to become a judge or a revenue agent.

This humble letter [8] puts us in vivid contact with the progress realized since Plato and Aristotle. But it is only fair to recognize that Alexander, in a certain way, was content with enlarging upon a principle defined by these philosophers. Thanks to this very extension it finally achieved its true meaning. The distinguishing characteristic of the Greeks for Plato and Aristotle, was the notion of *polis* (city-state), with the way of life and moral principles implied by the word. Every man, however, can become "Greek" since he comes within the *polis'* purview. With this end in view all that is needed is to educate the barbarians by integrating them into the city; this means on the practical level establishing cities which will be open to barbarians. Thus the idea of race gave way to the idea of civilization. The community was enlarged. There are no longer Greeks or barbarians, but "citizens." Only one last step remained: to conceive the idea of a single "city" which would take in all men, united by concord, in one and the same "civilized" community. Rome, imperial Rome, but above all Christian Rome, accomplished this achievement.

NOTES

1. Or of the world: Plato, *Tim.* 33 d, 34 b; *Stoicorum Veterum Gragmenta*, II, 186, 5.

2. As a matter of fact, although Hellenistic Greece never established a society comprised of all the Greek states, it was aware of the benefits of arbitration whether two contesting cities had recourse to a third, or to a sovereign. It is worth noting that, while granting the *civitates liberae et foederatae* (the free and united states) complete freedom in internal government, Rome never accorded them the right to take up arms against their neighbors under any pretext: cf. the excellent comments of Hugh Last in *Cambridge Ancient History*, XI, 436.

3. Here again the second Athenian Confederacy failed to reach a solution: cf. M. Cary in *Cambridge Ancient History*, VI, 73.

4. Aristotle through the words of Callisthenes? Or in his work *peri apoikiôn* (*On Colonies*)?

5. Erastosthenes in Strabo, I 66-67.

6. Again, the source is Erastothenes.

7. W. W. Tarn in *Cambridge Ancient History*, VI, 429-431; *Hellenistic Civilization*2 129-131; F. Cumont, *Fouilles de Doura Europos*, xliii - xliv, 341-344.

8. H. Lietzmann, *Griechische Papyri* (*Kl. T.*, XIV) n⁰ 4.